ACCOUNTING CONCEPTS FOR BEGINNER

Introduction of Accounting Concepts

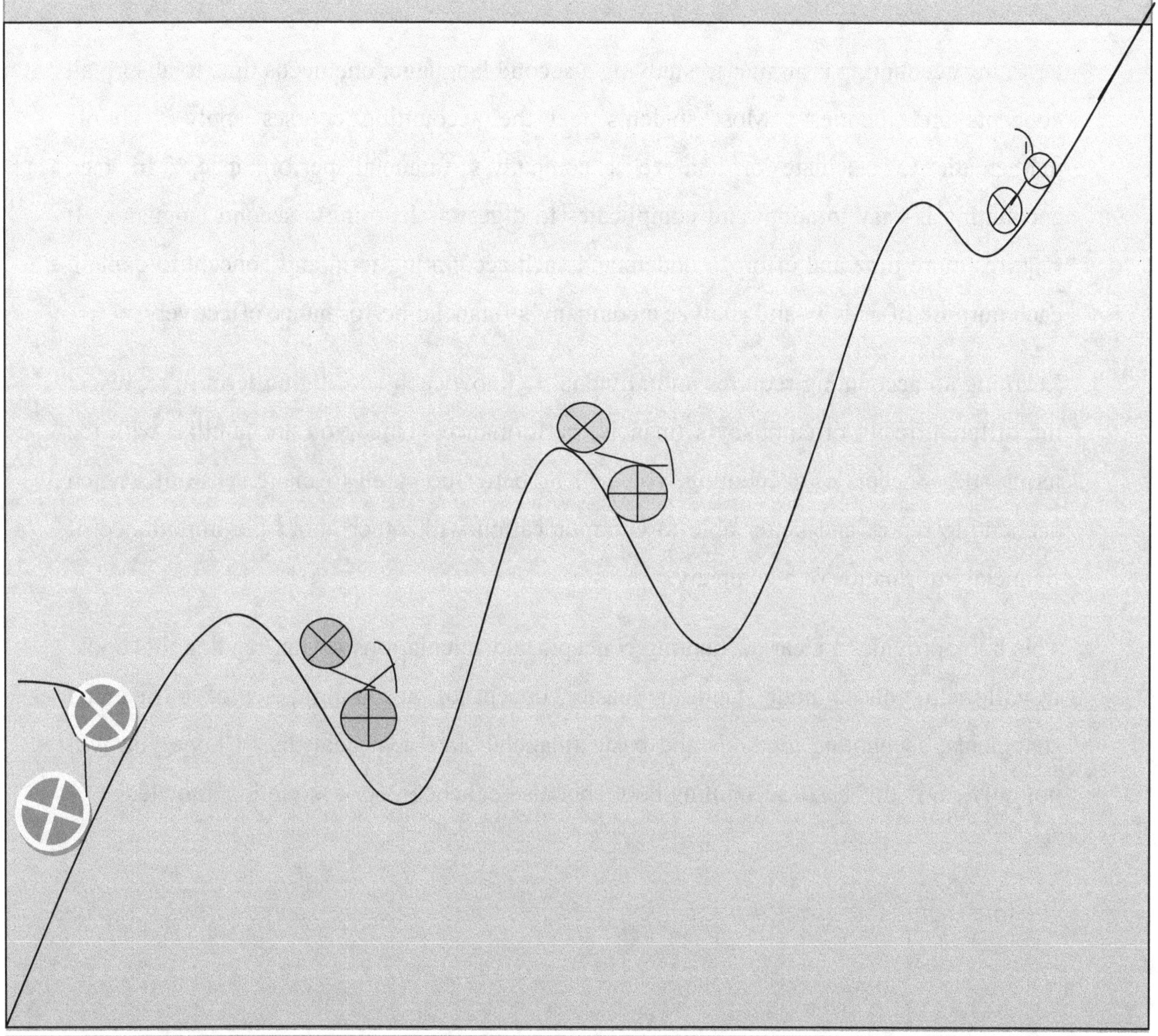

Dr. GRACER YUNG

INTRODUCTION

Learning accounting is similar to studying a second language; one needs time to absorb all concepts and theories. Most students feel the accounting courses apply a simple mathematic to calculate or analyze a company's financial performance. In fact, accounting is easy to adopt and complicates to digest as learning a second language. It requires more time and effort to understand each accounting term and concept to explain each purpose of activity and analyze a company's financial performance effectively.

Learning an accounting requires an individual to know each accounting term to represent the different result of company's financial performance. Once you are familiar with the terms and concepts of accounting, you will be better prepared to make sense of written accounting report and better able to communication with other about the importance of financial information of a company.

This book provides a clear accounting concepts and calculations. After reading this book, it will help you to understand the basic concept of accounting, set of a financial statements, accounting methods and basic financial statement analysis. I hope you will not only enjoy this basic accounting book, but also enhance your accounting knowledge.

TABLE OF CONTENT

CHAPTER ONE

ACCOUNTING TERMS

Before starting to understand a set of financial statements (income statement, owners' equity or stockholders' equity, balance sheet and statement of cash flow), it is important to know what is accounts and terms of accounting.

What is Accounts

Accounts are collection of financial information to record company transactions, such as customer purchases, payment to suppliers or creditors, repay debts, long-term or short-term investments, owner or shareholder equities, sale or service revenues, expenses and others. These financial records will create a set of financial statements that are summaries of all recorded transactions. For example [1] Income statement shows net profit. [2] Balance sheet indicates long-term and short-term assets /liabilities as well as owner / shareholder equity. [3] Statement of cash flow expresses the cash inflow and outflow that associated with operating activities, investment activities and financing activities. Moreover, each statement indicates different terms of activities. The most common accounting terms in each statement will discuss in following topic.

Accounting Terms of Income Statement

Income statement is also called as Profit and Loss Statement that explains the cash transactions from selling products or providing services. Under the income statement, it defines different transactions to calculate a company net profit or net income from revenues minus expenses. Net profit or net income represents a business's profit for a given year. If company produces revenues greater than expenses, company shows net income or net profit. On the other hand, if a company generates revenues less than expenses, company has negative income as net loss. Company may need to evaluate or redesign its business strategies for profitable operation.

$$\text{Revenue} > \text{Expenses} = \text{Net Income}$$

$$\text{Revenue} < \text{Expenses} = \text{Net Loss}$$

Reading the income statement of a company, it has some common terms of transactions to be used to record each activity. You have to understand the meaning of each transaction in order to help you easily to explain a company's financial performance and investigate an error from statements.

Common Terms of Income Statement

1] Revenues : It has two types of revenue from income statement, Sale revenues and service revenues.

>> *Sale Revenue* (for merchandising type of business) refers a company producing products for customers in order to generate the revenues.

>> *Service Revenue* (for service type of business) refers a company providing services to customers to generate the revenues. Example as Lawyers, Accountants, Doctors, etc.

2] Expenses : It reports into income statement as operating and non-operating expenses.

>> *Operating Expenses* incur to run a business operation which includes salaries, wages, advertising, utility, rent, supplies and more.

Common Terms of Operating Expenses

Salaries / Wages Expenses	Company pays to employees for producing products or providing services.
Advertising Expenses	Company pays to advertising company to promote the new products or services.
Utilities Expenses	Company pays for running the facility of business operation.
Rent Expenses	Company pays for the rental place for producing produces or providing services.
Supplies Expenses	Company pays for purchasing the inventories from suppliers.

>> *Non-operation Expenses* refer the expenses do not related to the company operation. The common one is interest expenses for money borrowing from banks or other financial institutions.

Common Terms of Non- Operating Expenses

Income Tax Expenses	Company pays to IRS for earned profits
Depreciation Expense	Company allocates the total capitalized assets to number of years
Interest Rate Expenses	company pays interest for money borrowed as non-operating expenses
Interest Rate Receivable	Company earns interest from investment as non-operating earning

Accounting Terms of Balance Sheet

Balance sheet includes three sections, [1] assets, [2] liabilities, and [3]owners' or shareholders' equity. Preparing the balance sheet, it requires a Basic Accounting Equation, which is *Assets = Liabilities + Owners' equity or Shareholder's equity*. Let us to define each session of the balance sheet.

First Session of Balance Sheet
Current Assets and Non-Current Assets
Common Terms of Current Assets – Assets Can Be Liquidated Within A Year :

Cash	Cash is available on hand
Accounts receivable	Company expects the amount will be received for the services provided or merchandise to sale to customers on credit within the short period of time (less than a year).
Notes receivable	It is a written promise to specified a person to receive a certain amount of money at a certain time and interest
Inventory	Goods or merchandises are available to be sold to customers.
Short-term investments	Company investments are maturity within a year

Common Terms of Non-Current Assets – Assets Invested to Operate the Business and Assets Can Be Liquidated More Than A Year

Notes Receivable	Company holds a written promissory note from another party. They sign a written promise to repay the amount to company.
Plan, Property and Equipment (PP & E)	Fixed assets invest in a business to generate the profit.
Accumulated depreciation	Investments amount allocate in estimated life of long-term assets. The amount of invested assets will be subtracted to determine the book value in current year.

Second Session of Balance Sheet
Current liabilities and Non-Current Liabilities

Liabilities are amount of company obligation to repay the debt borrowed. Liabilities can be defined as current and non-current liabilities under the second session of balance sheet.

Common Terms Of Current Liabilities – liabilities is obligated to pay within a year

Accounts Payable	Company obligates to pay for purchasing produces or providing services.
Notes Payable (current)	Company issues promissory note to exchange either cash or others with obligation to pay with interest.
Current Notes Payable as Long Term Debt	Company incurs debt for long-term investments. The amount of current due from long-term debt reduces the long-term obligation. Mortgage is one of an example.

Common Terms Of Non-Current liabilities

Notes Payable (Non-Current)	Company issues promissory note with obligation to pay with interest after a year.
Long-Term Liabilities	Company borrows money to finance or operate a business

Common Terms of Stockholders' Equity or Owners' Equity

Stockholder's Equity	Investors invest into a company with certain percent of interest of a company. The example with ending retained earnings are reported under Stockholders' equity in the statement of balance sheet	* Example Beginning Retained Earnings + Net Income - Dividend ------------------------------------- = Ending Retained Earnings
OR		
Owners' Equity	Owners invest their capital to a company. The example with ending owners' equity are reported under Owners' equity in the statement of balance sheet.	* Example Beginning Owners' Equity + Capital Investment - Withdrawal + Net Income ------------------------------------- = Ending Owners' Equity

* it will talk about more in next chapter

STATEMENT OF CASH FLOW

Statement of cash flow is one of the main financial statements to reveal company cash inflows and outflows from operating, investing and financial activities. In addition, these three sections will explore the cash inflow and outflow from normal operation such as revenues and cash operating.

Three Sections Activities from Statement of Cash Flow

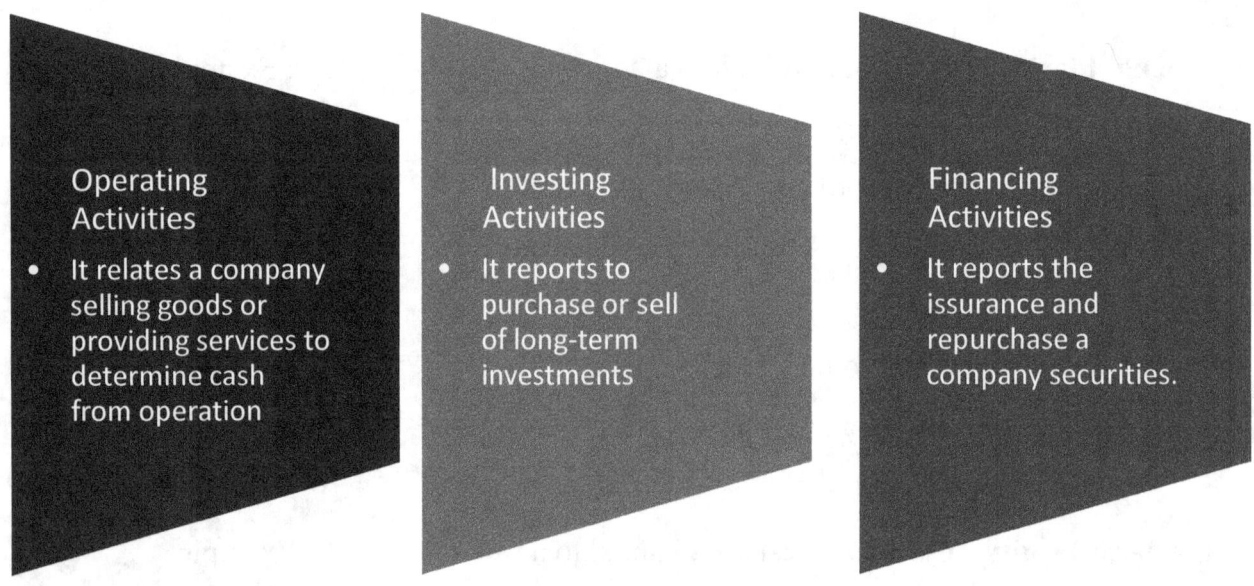

Operating Activities
- It relates a company selling goods or providing services to determine cash from operation

Investing Activities
- It reports to purchase or sell of long-term investments

Financing Activities
- It reports the issurance and repurchase a company securities.

Each activity from the statement of cash flow is prepared under the accrual basis (it will talk about more in other chapter). In fact, statement of cash flow will not result the same income from income statement. The reason is that the revenue reported that may not be been collected or the expenses may not be paid. In addition, the statement of cash flow of each activity has integrated all information from income statement and balance sheet.

Diagram of Statement of Cash Flow

[1] Operating Activities

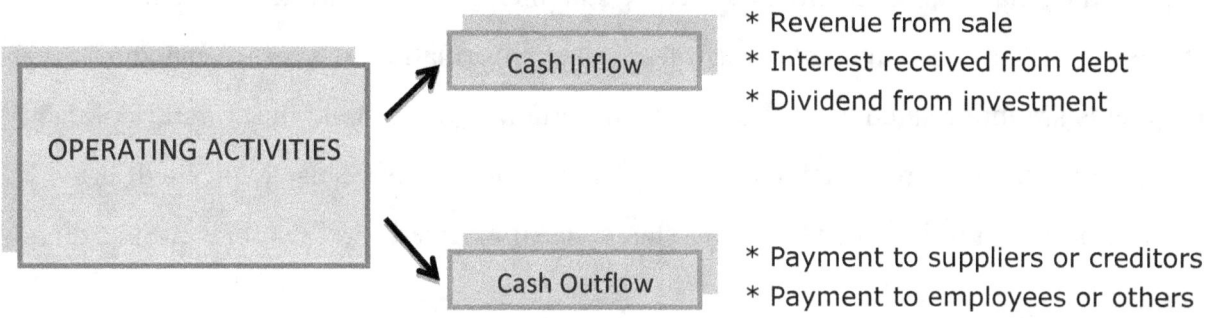

OPERATING ACTIVITIES

Cash Inflow
* Revenue from sale
* Interest received from debt
* Dividend from investment

Cash Outflow
* Payment to suppliers or creditors
* Payment to employees or others

[2] Investing Activities

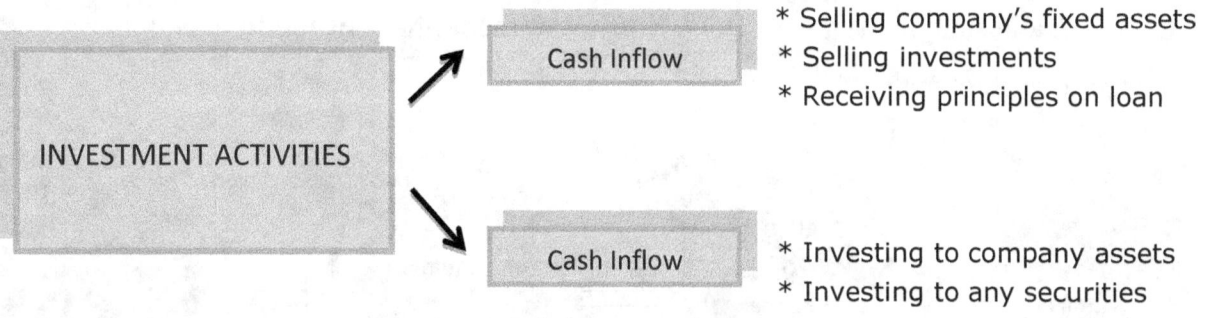

INVESTMENT ACTIVITIES

Cash Inflow
* Selling company's fixed assets
* Selling investments
* Receiving principles on loan

Cash Inflow
* Investing to company assets
* Investing to any securities

[3] Financing activities

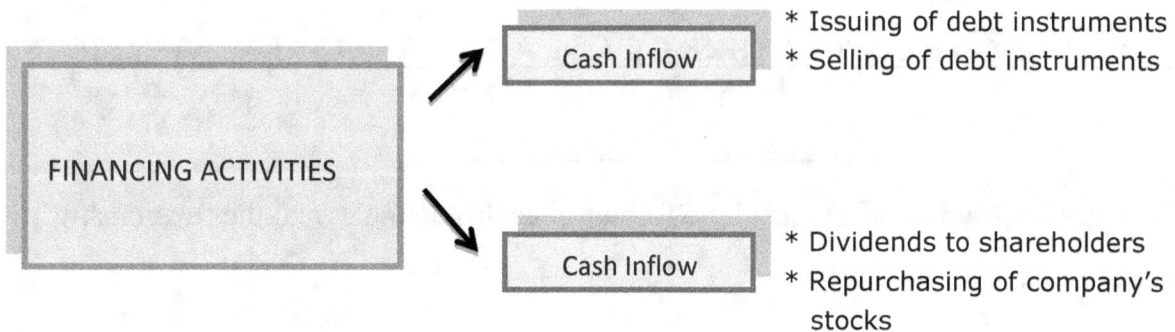

FINANCING ACTIVITIES

Cash Inflow
* Issuing of debt instruments
* Selling of debt instruments

Cash Inflow
* Dividends to shareholders
* Repurchasing of company's stocks

CHAPTER TWO

SET OF FINANCIAL STATEMENTS

A set of financial statements include income statement, balance sheet, statement of retained earnings and statement of cash flow. The information of a set of financial statements are interrelated each other. It is important to understand the structure of each statement and activity reported to a set of financial statements. This chapter will provide detail information of income statement, statement of retained earnings, balance sheet and statement of cash flow.

SET OF FINANCIAL STATEMENTS

Income statement will be prepared first, following with statement of retained earnings, balance sheet, and statement of cash flow. Each statement provides the financial data interrelated to each other.

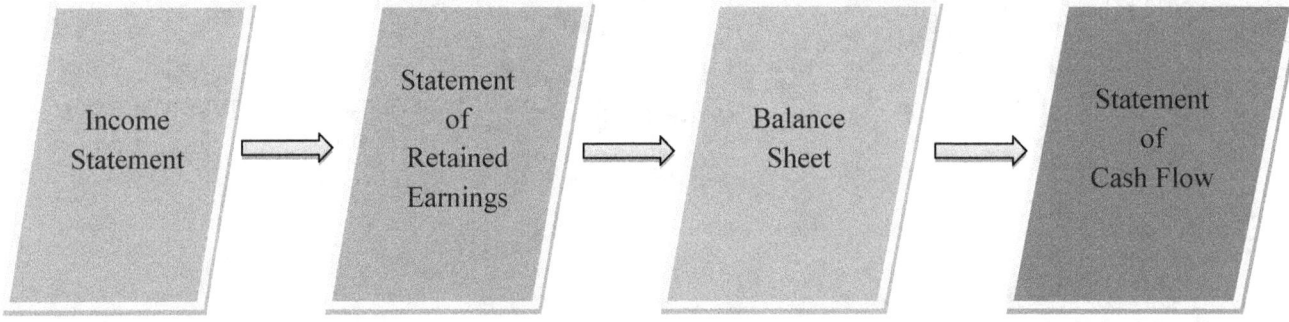

<u>EXPLORING THE STRUCTURE OF A SET OF FINANCIAL STATEMENTS</u>

<u>FINANCIAL STATEMNT</u>

This chapter helps you to understand the format of each statement, and the relationship between of financial statements.

INCOME STATEMENT

Income statement is sometimes referred to as the profit and loss statement (P & L) to record company profitability. Income statement shows the earned revenue, and expenses to determine the gain and loss. If company can generate the revenues greater than the expenses, a company shows the net income. On the other hand, if a company generates the revenues less than the expenses, it shows the net loss.

However, company's ability to operate profitably business is important to external users (person does not belong to organization) and internal users (person related to organization) for major decision-making.

Diagram of Internal and External Users

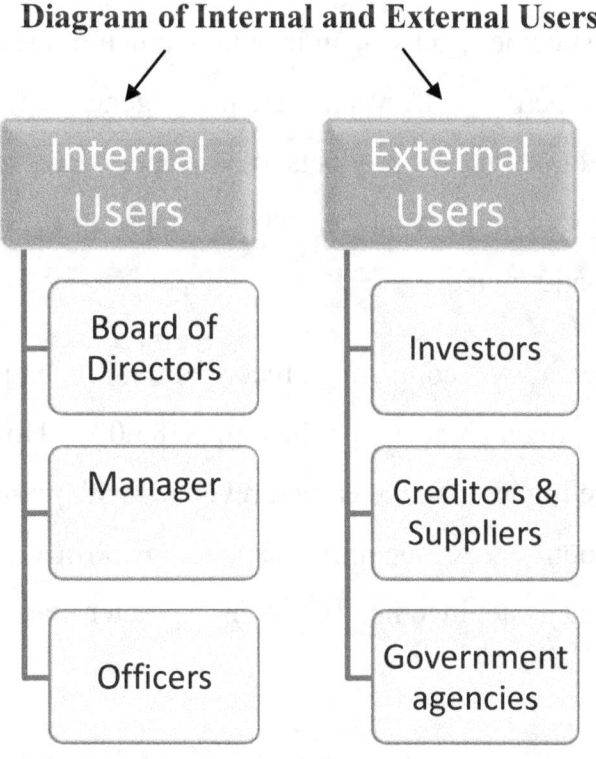

Format of Income Statement

Income statement generally is classified (1) revenues (2) expenses that provide information of a company operating performance over a period of time. It is important to understand the concept, and theory of income statement.

	[Company A]		[Company B]	
REVENUES	Revenues	$500,000	Revenues	$500,000
-- EXPENSES	Expenses	(15,000)	Expenses	(600,000)
NET INCOME / LOSS	Net Income	$485,000	Net Loss	($100,000)

Basically, the income statement get you an idea how much money the company generated (revenue), and spent (expenses). *Revenue*s are profit generate from business operation for providing services or selling the products to customers. *Expenses* relate to operate the business in order to produce the revenues, such as wages, utilities, rental expenses, office supplies, maintenance and more.

From the table indicated above, company A recorded total revenues $500,000 and expenses $15,000 to giving a company net income $485,000. However, Company B shows the expenses are higher than the earned revenues with net loss $100,000. In the other words, if net amount of revenue minus expenses is positive, the bottom line of the profit and loss is labeled as net income. If expenses greater than earned revenue, company shows net loss.

The following example of income statement shows the detail calculation of net income or net loss.

Prepare Basic Income Statement

Income Statement
ABC Company
December 31, 20xx

Revenue :		
Sale/service revenue		**$200,000**
Expenses:		
Office supplies expenses	($ 1,300)	
Advertising expenses	(6,000)	
Depreciation expenses	(1,000)	
Rental expenses	(10,000)	
Utilities expenses	(2,000)	
Salaries and wages expenses	(5,000)	
Total Expenses		($ 25,300)
Net Income		**$174,700**

The example of income statement shows the net income $174,700 = Revenue $200,000 – total expenses $25,300. This income statement is telling us that a company is making the profit from the revenue minus all expenses. In other word, revenue is greater than expenses.

Format of Statement of Retained Earnings

Statement of retained earnings indicates the total of residual income in a company at the end of accounting period. Most companies retain or set aside the residual income in order to reinvest in its core business projects, other investments or pay dividends. However, statement of retained earnings can be affected based on company profitability. If a company generates high satisfactory profit, the ending retained earning can be higher. Company will have more residual income retained for any other future investments, projects, or dividend distribution.

In addition, the ending retained earnings will apply to balance sheet under Stockholders' Equity or Owners' Equity to determine the total equities on hand of a company at the end of accounting period. The following example shows the format of statement of retained earnings for stockholders' equity and owners' equity. *For stockholders' equity* is starting with beginning retained earnings plus net income and minus dividend to determine the ending retained earnings. *For owners' equity* is starting with beginning of owners' capital plus capital investments, plus net income, and subtract owners' withdrawal to determine the ending of owner's equity.

Statement of Retained Earnings for Stockholders' Equity

Beginning Retained Earning	**Beginning Retained Earning**	**$400,000**
+ Net Income	**+ Net Income**	**174,700**
- Dividend	**- Dividend**	**(50,000)**
= Ending Retained Earning	**= Ending Retained Earning**	**$524,700**

Explanation the Terms of Statement of Retained Earnings in Stockholders' Equity

(1) *Beginning Retained Earning* – beginning retained earnings are carrying forward the ending balance from previously accounting period

(2) *Net Income* – Net income is from the bottom of income statement

(3) *Dividend* – dividend paid to shareholders

(4) *Ending Retained Earning* = Beginning Retained Earning + Net Income – Dividend

From the example above, the ending retained earning shows the totally of $524,700. It increased by $124,700 ($524,000 - $ 400,000) from adding net income and subtracting paid dividend. It indicates that company generates more profit and more residual income on hand.

Statement of Retained Earnings for Owners' Equity

Beginning Owners' Equity	**Beginning Owners' Equity**	**$400,000**
+ **Owner's capital investment**	+ **owner's capital investment**	**100,000**
+ **Net Income**	+ **Net Income**	**174,700**
- **Owners' Withdrawal**	- **Owners' Withdrawal**	**(80,000)**
= **Ending Owners' Equity**	= **Ending Owners' Equity**	**$594,700**

Explanation the Terms of Statement of Retained Earnings in Owners' Equity

(1) *Beginning Owners' Equity* – Beginning owners' equity is carrying forward ending balance from previously accounting period

(2) *Owner's capital investment* – it shows owner's investment to company during this accounting period

(3) *Net Income* – it is from the bottom of income statement

(3) *Owners' Withdrawal* – Owner withdrawal as personal expenses

(4) *Ending Owners' Equity* = Beginning Retained Earning+ Owner's capital investment + Net Income – withdrawal

From the example above, the ending owners' equity is increasing by $194,700 based on the additional capital investment, and net income after owners' withdrawal.

Format of Balance Sheet

Balance sheet is used to summarize a company's assets, liabilities and shareholders' equity or owners' equity at a specific point in time. It is divided into three segments in order to give investors or owners to see the insight of company assets they own, liabilities they owe and shareholders' or owners' equity invest to a company. Each segment of the balance sheet will have many accounts to show the company current and non-current assets and liabilities as well as the shareholders or owners' equity.

Under the balance sheet, assets are listed fist, and followed by liabilities and stockholder's equity or owner's equity. When you prepare the balance sheet, the basic equation must be followed; **Assets = Liabilities + Shareholders' Equity**.

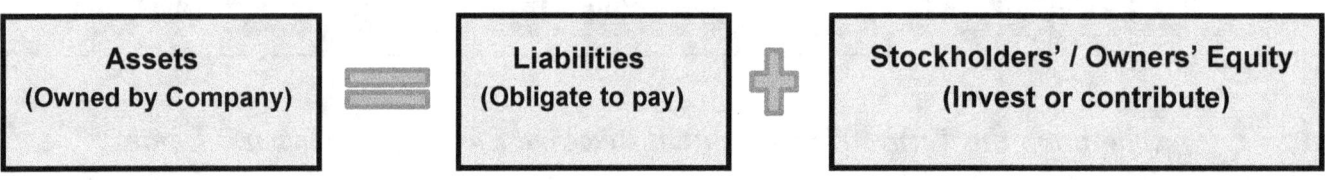

Assets from the balance sheet can be identified into short-term assets and long-term assets. Recalled from the accounting terms of balance sheet, short-term assets can be liquidated within a year to converting into cash to pay current liabilities. It is including cash, accounts receivable, notes receivable, inventories and other short-term investments. Long-term assets require more than a year to convert into cash that are including plan, equipment and property (PP&E) and others long term investments.

Common Short-Terms and Long-Terms Transactions in Statement of Balance Sheet

Definition of Current Assets

Current Assets (Current Assets Can Be Converted Within a Year to Pay Current Liabilities)	
Cash	It includes money, coins, checks and notes
Accounts Receivable	Company sales of products or provides services on credit, customers will pay based on the term or payment agreement. Company also expects to receive or collects cash or outstanding balance from customers with short period of time.
Inventory	It includes raw materials, work-in-process and finished goods. When company has physical counts, they should include all of them to determine the value of inventory on hand. 1] Raw materials need to make finish products 2] Work-in-process refers partially completed, but not the entire finished products. 3] Finished goods are final products that are ready to sell in the market.
Short-term investments	Company invests short-term investments with high liquidation. Company expects to covert cash within a year.

Definition of Non-Current Assets

Non-Current Assets (Non-current Assets will be used for business operation more than a year)	
Notes Receivable (Long-Term)	A promissory note obligates to pay with principle and interest more than a year.
Property, Plant and Equipment (PP&E)	Company invests fixed assets as property, plant and equipment to intent operating business. Costs of long-term investments will be allocated in the number of years as depreciation expenses. It will take more than a year to covert or sale to be cash.
Long Term Investments	Investments invest into company that needs more than a year to liquidate to be cash

Definition of Stockholders' Equity

Stockholders' Equity (Stockholders invest to company and they are the owner of company)	
Common Stock	Stockholders invest to company to exchange certain percentage of company stocks
Retained Earnings	It is part of company's net profit and part of common shares' equity

Definition of Owners' Equity

Owners' Equity (Owners invest their capital to business)	
Capital	Owners invest to business as owners capital
Withdrawal	Owners withdraw from owners' account as personal expenses.
Net profit	It also includes into the owners' equity to determine the ending owners' equity.

Each section of component from statement of balance sheet clearly defines a type of transaction. From the top of balance sheet, company will record short-term and long-term assets and liabilities. Following at the bottom of balance sheet, it will record either stockholders equity or owners' equity, which depends on a form of organization. If shareholders own certain percentage of a company, balance sheet will show number of outstanding common shares under the section of stockholders' equity. On the other hand, if owners of a business invest or withdraw from a company, it will record into their investment accounts under the section of owners' equity.

Following example of the statement of balance sheet shows a clear picture to record each transaction into each section (Assets, Liabilities and Stockholders' Equity or Owners' Equity). It also addresses the importance of basic accounting equation from the statement of balance sheet. The total asset with $869,845* is equal to the total liabilities $145,000** and total stockholders' equity $724,700**.

BALANCE SHEET
ABC Company
December 31, 20XX

	ASSETS	
Cash		$ 627,845
Account Receivable		80,000
Inventories		50,000
Note Receivable		20,000
Prepaid expenses		12,000
Equipment (net)		80,000
Total Asset		**$ 869,845 ***
	LIABILITIES	
Account Payable		$ 35,000
Note Payable		10,000
Short-term Debt		30,000
Long-term Debt		70,000
Total Liabilities		**$145,000 ****
	STOCKHOLDER'S EQUITY	
Common Shares		$ 200,000
Retained Earning		524,700
Total Stockholder's Equity		**$ 724,700 ****
Total Liabilities and Stockholder's Equity		**$ 869,845 ***

Recalling the basic accounting equation applied to stockholders' equity and owners' equity as follows:

$$ASSETS = LIABILITIES + \underline{\textit{STOCKHOLDERS' EQUITY}}$$

OR

$$ASSETS = LIABILITIES + \underline{\textit{OWNERS' EQUITY}}$$

Example of Stockholders' Equity and Owners' Equity

Owner's equity :	Stockholder's equity:
Beginning Owners' equity + owners investment + net income – owners' drawing = Ending Owner's equity *Example :*	*Beginning Retained Earning + Net Income – Dividend = Ending Retained Earnings:* *Example :*
Beginning owner's equity $400,000 + Owner's Investment 56,000 + Net Income 174,700 - Owner's drawing (106,000) = Ending owner's equity $524,700	Beginning Retained Earnings $400,000 + Net Income 174,700 - Dividend (50,000) = Ending Retained Earnings $524,700
The ending owners' equity show at the bottom of balance sheet under owners' equity:	**The ending retained earnings show at the bottom of balance sheet under stockholders' equity :** Stockholder's equity :
Owner's equity : Owner's equity $524,700 Total Owner's equity $524,700	Common shares $200,000 Retained Earnings 524,700 Total Stockholder's equity $724,700

Sometime you might find a statement of balance sheet either with stockholders' equity or owners' equity at the bottom of statement. As we mentioned previously, *Owners' equity* is owners' capital invested in the business. The ending balance of owner's equity = beginning of owners' equity + capital investment + net income – owners' drawing. However, *stockholders' equity* is investments from the investors in exchange certain percentage of company's common stocks. In other words, stockholders are a part of the company owners with certain percent of ownership of company. Stockholders' equity also can be determined from Total Assets – Total Liabilities.

Partial Balance Sheet of Stockholders' Equity and Owner's Equity

STOCKHOLDER'S EQUITY	
Stockholders' Equity	
Common Stock	$ 200,000
Retain Earning	524,700
Total Stockholder's Equity	*$ 724,700*

ONWER'S EQUITY	
Owners' Equity	
Owners' Equity	524,700
Total Owners' Equity	*$ 524,700*

The example above shows the partial financial information of stockholders equity and owners' equity with the different results. Stockholders' equity has total equity $724,700 including the total outstanding common stock value. Owners' equity has total $524,700 with owners' capital only.

After discussing the income statement and balance sheet, the other related financial statement is statement of Cash flow. It is one of the main financial statements to report the cash inflow and outflow in business activities. The cash flow transactions divided into three components that include operation activities, investing activities, and financing activities. Also, the net change from statement of cash flow should equal to the change in a company's cash during the reporting period in balance sheet.

[1] Operating activities – converting the actitives reported on the income statement .

[2] Investing activity – reporting the purchase and sale of long-term investments.

[3] Financing activity – reporting the issuance and repurchases of the company's own bonds and stocks, and the payment of dividends.

Statement of Cash Flow

Operating Activities		
Cash received from customers		$777,845
Cash from supplies expenses	($ 1,300)	
Cash from advertising expenses	(6,000)	
Cash paid for rental expenses	(10,000)	
Cash paid for utilities expenses	(2,000)	
Cash paid for salaries / wages	(5,000)	(24,300)
Cash provided by operating activities		$753,545
Investing Activities		
Purchased equipment	($80,000)	
Cash provided by investing activities		($80,000)
Financing Activities		
Paid dividend	($200,000)	
Cash provided by financing activities		($200,000)
Beginning Cash		0.00
Ending Cash		$627,845

The financial informaiton from statement of cash flow is associated with income statement and balance sheet. It is important to know that the ending cash must be equal to cash from balance sheet. As you can see the total ending cash with $627,845 can be found from the top of balance sheet as cash under current assets. See the partical Balance Sheet and Partical statement of cash flow as follows:

Partial Balance Sheet (From the top of Balance Sheet)	
Current Assets	
Cash	$627,845

Partial Statement of Cash Flow (From the bottom of Statement of Cash Flow)	
Ending Cash	$627,845

CHAPTER THREE

VARIOUS ACCOUNTING METHODS

This chapter will explore more accounting methods to record company transactions. It is including (1) cash basis, (2) accrual basis, (3) Inventory methods (Last-in-first-out and first-in-first-out), (4) periodic and perpetual system, and (5) depreciation methods. Those methods are helpful for a company to analyze its financial status for decision-making.

First, we will discuss cash basis and accrual basis. What is different between the cash basis and accrual basis and how does it affect the financial statement?

CASH BASIS ACCOUNTING

Cash basis is used to record income and expenses when is received or paid out. However, cash basis does not conform to GAAP (General Accepted Accounting Principle).

ACCRUAL BASIS ACCOUNTING

Based on accrual basis, companies are required to record each transaction when is incurred. Accrual basis might also require lot of adjustments, since recorded revenue may not receive or expenses may not pay. In addition, it might create a bad debt of a company, if outstanding accounts receivable cannot collect from customers.

The following example shows the year of 2012 by using the cash basis with net loss $-2,000 and accrual basis with net income by $48, 000. In the follow year of 2013, the cash basis indicates the net income has $50,000 and accrual basis has zero balance.

As mentioned before, accrual basis records all transactions as it occurred, and cash basis only records the cash received and expenses paid. It is important to familiar with each accounting method. It might have significant effects in the financial statements.

.

Comparative of Cash Basis and Accrual Basis Accounting

Example: Company sold 100 units of small machines at $ 500 per unit in 2012. Also, company expensed $200, and the remaining outstanding balance $4,800 will be received next 2013.

2012		2012	
Cash Basis		*Accrual Basis*	
Cash	$0.00	Cash	$50,000
Expenses	2,000	Expenses	2,000
Net Loss	**$-2,000**	**Net income**	**$48,000**

2013		2013	
Cash Basis		*Accrual Basis*	
Cash	$50,000	Cash	0.00
Expense	0.00	Expenses	0.00
Net Income	**$50,000**	**Net Income**	**0.00**

CASH FLOW ASSUMPTION

When a company operates its business as merchandising or retailing, it is important to establish a good inventory control systems to monitor each type of inventory on hand. Two common types of inventory control systems include First-in, First-out (FIFO) and Last-in, First-out (LIFO). Both methods are used to measure a company's ending inventory and cost flow of inventory or cost of goods sold. If company operates its business with high volumes of inventory, it needs to determine a type of inventory methods (FIFO or LIFO) to value its ending inventory and cost of goods sold. In fact, both methods use to evaluate the process of assigning value of raw materials, work-in-process and finished goods on financial statements.

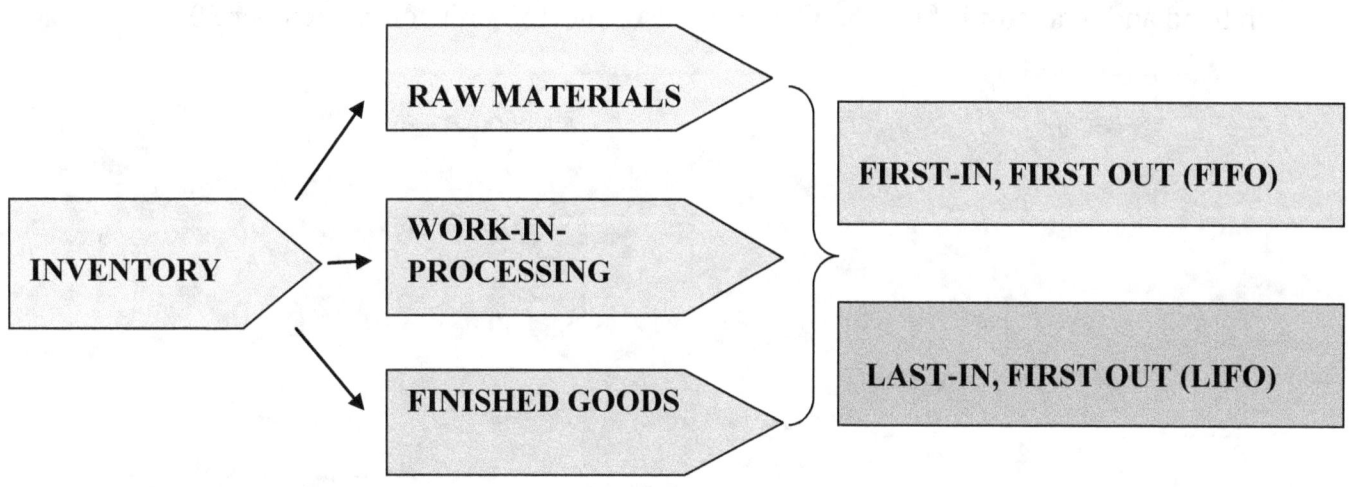

First-In, First-Out (FIFO) Method

First-In, First-Out is one of the methods commonly used to calculate the value of inventory on hand and the cost of goods sold during the accounting period. This method assumes the inventory purchased first that sold first, and newer inventory remains unsold. However, costs of older inventory assign to cost of goods sold and newer inventory assign to ending inventories.

The following example illustrates the calculation of ending inventory and cost of goods sold under FIFO method:

Example :

Following information uses to calculate the value of inventory on hand and cost of goods sold during September by using the *FIFO method*. Company has 350 units as inventory on hand and total cost is $6,285. Company also sold 150 units on September 30.

Sept 1	Beginning Inventory	100 units	$10.00 per unit	$1,000
3	Purchase	90 units	$19.00 per unit	$1,710
15	Purchase	85 units	$20.00 per unit	$1,700
20	Purchase	75 units	$25.00 per unit	$1,875
		Total Units 350		Total Cost $6,285

First-In, First-Out (FIFO)

Company sold 150 units by applying FIFO method:

Step 1: Calculate the Ending Inventory

Step 2 : Calculate the Cost of Goods Sold

Calculate the Ending Inventory
First-In, First-Out (FIFO)

Sept 3	**40 units**	**$19.00**	**$ 760.00**
Sept 15	85 units	$20.00	$1,700.00
Sept 20	75 units	$25.00	$1,875.00
Ending Inventory			***$4,335.00***

From the calculation above with FIFO method, company has beginning inventory 100 units and other 50 units from September 3 is picked with total 150 units together to sell to customers. Now, it only has remaining 40 units on September 3. Company does not need to touch the inventories on September 15 and 20, since it only sold 150 units by applying FIFO method.

Calculate the cost of goods sold
First-In, First-Out (FIFO)

Cost of Goods Available for Sale (Total Units)	$6, 285.00
Less ; Ending Inventory	4, 335.00
Cost of Goods Sold	**$1,950.00**

After calculating the ending inventory, you can determine the cost of goods sold (COGS). Cost of goods sold is the costs to create the products to sells. It directly ties to the production of products in order to generate revenue. According to the calculation, company has total cost of goods available for sale is $6,285.00 and ending inventory on hand $4,335.00. After subtracting the ending inventory from cost of good available for sale, the total cost of goods sold is $1,950.00.

Last-In, First-Out (LIFO) Method

It is also a one of the methods commonly used in the valuation of inventory on hand at the end of a period and the cost of goods sold during the period. LIFO assumes the most latest purchased products is sold first. LIFO assigns the cost of newer inventory to cost of goods sold and cost of older inventory to ending inventory account.

Here, we will use the pervious information to determine the cost of goods sold and ending inventory by using LIFO method. From the calculation below with LIFO method, a company started with the lasted inventory 75 units from September 20 and other 75 units from September 15 to add it up the total 150 units to sell to customers. Now, it only has remaining 10 units on September 15. However, September 3 and beginning of inventory is remaining the same. In the other words, company does not need to touch the inventories on September 3 and beginning inventory, since it only sold 150 units by applying LIFO method.

The following example illustrates the calculation of ending inventory and cost of goods sold under LIFO method. You will see the difference between LIFO and FIFO method.

Example :

The following information is used to calculate the value of inventory on hand and cost of goods sold during September by using the *LIFO method*. Company has 350 units as inventories on hand and total cost is $6,825. Also, company sold 150 units on September 30.

Sept 1	Beginning Inventory	100 units	$10.00 per unit	$1,000
3	Purchase	90 units	$19.00 per unit	$1,710
15	Purchase	85 units	$20.00 per unit	$1,700
20	Purchase	75 units	$25.00 per unit	$1,875
		Total Units 350		Total Cost $6,825

Company sold 150 units by applying LIFO method. The procedure is same as FIFO.

Step 1 : Calculate the Ending Inventory

Step 2: Calculate the Cost of goods sold

Calculate the Ending Inventory (LIFO)

Sept 15	10 units	$20.00	$ 200.00
Sept 3	90 units	$19.00	$1,710.00
Beginning Inventory	100 units	$10.00	$1,000.00
Ending Inventory			**$2,910.00**

Calculate Cost of Goods Sold (LIFO)

Cost of Goods Available for Sale (Total Units)	$6, 825.00
Less ; Ending Inventory	2,910.00
Cost of Goods Sold	**$3,915.00**

After calculating the ending inventory by using the LIFO method, you can determine cost of goods sold (COGS). As mentioned before, cost of goods sold is the costs to create the products to sells. It is directly tied to the production of products in order to generate revenue. According to the calculation, company has total cost of good available for sale is $6,825.00 and ending inventory on hand $2,910.00. After subtracting the ending inventory from cost of good available for sale, the total cost of goods sold is $3,915.00

Comparative of FIFO and LIFO Method

	FIFO	LIFO
Cost of Goods Available for Sale (Total Units)	$6,825.00	$6,825.00
Less ; Ending Inventory	4,335.00	2,910.00
Cost of Goods Sold	2,490.00	3,915.00

As the table above, the cost of goods available for sale is same for both methods. However, FIFO shows the ending inventory higher than the LIFO and Cost of goods sold as expense is lower than the LIFO. In the other words, company by using the FIFO method has higher net profit than the LIFO. If company has 35% income tax, company with FIFO method will pay more than LIFO method. See the income statement below.

Example : Assuming a company has total revenue $80,000. The cost of goods sold will be used to determine the net income from FIFO and LIFO method.

FIFO and LIFO Method Comparison

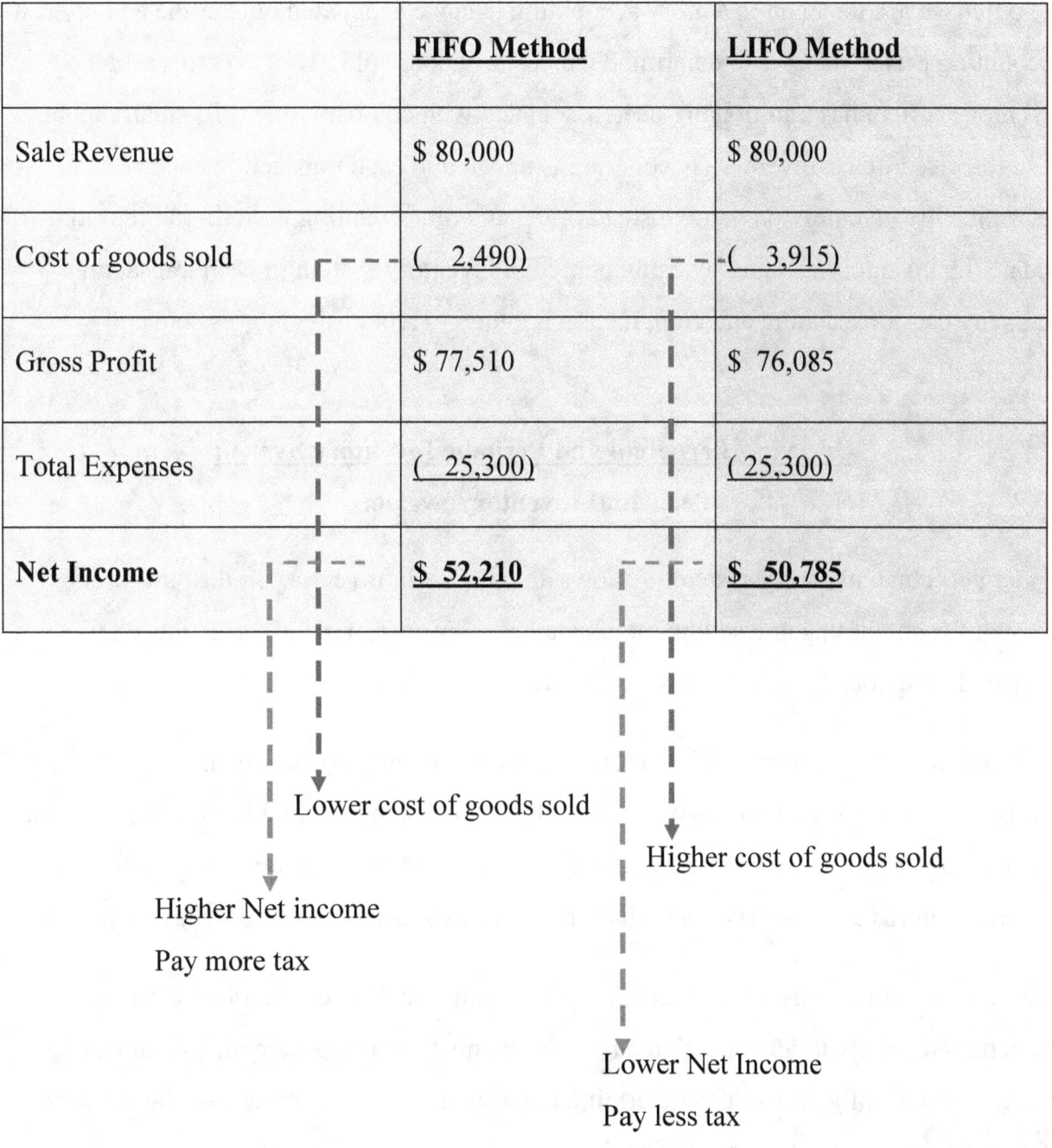

	FIFO Method	LIFO Method
Sale Revenue	$ 80,000	$ 80,000
Cost of goods sold	(2,490)	(3,915)
Gross Profit	$ 77,510	$ 76,085
Total Expenses	(25,300)	(25,300)
Net Income	**$ 52,210**	**$ 50,785**

Lower cost of goods sold

Higher cost of goods sold

Higher Net income

Pay more tax

Lower Net Income

Pay less tax

Perpetual and Periodic Inventory System

Company may use either perpetual or periodic inventory system to account for inventory. Differentiate between perpetual or periodic inventory system shows the recording for inventories on hand. Under periodic inventory system, merchandise purchases record in the purchase account, and inventory accounting balance is updated only at the end of each accounting period in order to determine the cost of goods sold. However, perpetual inventory system has traditionally been associated with company that sells small number of high-priced items, inventory accounting is updated in each transaction occurred to determine the inventory on hand, instead of the end of accounting period. In order to update the inventory on hand by using perpetual inventory system in each transaction, company uses of scanning and computer technology to report inventories sold and purchased.

Overview Perpetual and Periodic Inventory System
Perpetual Inventory System

Under perpetual inventory system, it shows all changes in inventory in the "inventory" account for purchasing and selling merchandises. However, purchase accounts do use in a perpetual inventory system to determent inventories on hand.

As mentioned above, perpetual inventory system continually updates its inventory records and provides up-to-date inventory balance information on hand. In addition, the inventory account balance is immediately recognized to accurate in the inventory account by sales and sales returns and purchases, purchase returns and allowance, and purchase discounts.

Example: Company has sale revenue $100,000 with sale discount $2,000. Customer also has returned item with $5,000. You have to remember, by using perpetual inventory system, the cost of goods sold is determined in each transaction. After calculated the cost of goods sold, you needs to determine the net income by taking several steps as follows:

Step 1 : Calculate net sale from sale revenue minus sale return and allowance, and sale discount

Step 2: Calculate gross profit from net sale minus cost of goods sold

Step 3 : Calculate net income from gross profit minus all expenses

Income Statement with Perpetual Inventory System

XYZ Company
Income Statement
December 31, 201X

Sale Revenue		$100,000
Less: Sale Return and Allowance	($ 5,000)	
Sale Discount	(2,000)	(7,000)
Net Sale		93,000
Cost of goods sold		35,000
Gross Profit		58,000
Expenses		30,000
Net Income		**$28,000**

Step 1

Step 2

Step 3

By using a perpetual inventory system, it is important to understand how to record each transaction. The following examples show the journal entries in a perpetual inventory system.

Perpetual Inventory System Journal Entries

[1] Company records a purchase of $3,000 of merchandise from supplier A on account:

	Debit	Credit
Inventory	3,000	
Accounts payable		3,000

This transaction indicates that company purchased merchandises on credit and will pay later. This transaction increases company liabilities by $3,000. When it paid, liabilities decrease $3,000 and decrease cash by $3,000. Since company uses perpetual inventory system, inventor on hand will update from this journal entry.

[2] Company records $ 800 of freight cost associated with the delivery of inventory:

	Debit	Credit
Inventory	800	
Accounts payable		800

Based on this transaction, company includes the freight cost into the inventory. It shows the inventory cost increased with the delivery cost of inventory.

[3] Company records a sale of inventory for $10,000 on credit, and cost of production cost is $ 4,000:

	Debit	Credit
Accounts receivable	10,000	
Revenue		10,000
Cost of goods sold	4,000	
Inventory		4,000

These transactions indicate company sold the merchandise with $10,000 on credit. Company will receives the outstanding balance from customers within short period of time. Company also increases revenue with the same amount $10,000. However, the sale revenue associated with cost of goods sold as a company expenses to manufactory the finished merchandise to customers for $4,000. It also decrease inventory by $4,000. According to this sale transaction, company shows the Gross profit with $6,000 after subtracting the cost of goods sold from sale revenue ($10,000 - $4,000).

[4] Company records a return purchased inventory of $ 600

	Debit	Credit
Account Payable	600	
Inventory		600

This transaction shows a company has returned purchase inventory of $600. It reduces company liability and decrease inventory as the same amount.

Periodic Inventory System

Periodic inventory system uses to keep the inventory balance at the same value from the beginning of year. However, ending inventory balance will be updated with a physical count to determine the cost of goods sold at the end of accounting period.

Under the periodic inventory system, all purchases made between physical inventory counts records in purchases account. When a physical inventory count is done, it shifts the balance in the purchases account into the inventory account, which in turn is adjusted to match the cost of the ending inventory

Example: Company has sale revenue $100,000 with sale discount $2,000. Customer also has returned item with $5,000. In addition, Company has beginning inventory of $1,000, merchandise purchases $45,000, purchase return $5,000, purchases discount $2,000, and

$1,500 Freight cost. Its physical inventory count reveals an ending inventory cost of $5,500. Based on periodic inventory system, it needs to take more steps to determine the cost of goods sold and net income compared with perpetual inventory system.

Step 1 : Sale Revenue subtracts the Sale Return and Allowance, and Sale Discount to arrive Net Sale

Step 2: Calculate the Cost of Goods Sold:

- ✓ Determine the beginning inventory
- ✓ Add : Purchased merchandise within the period of accounting period
- ✓ Subtract: Purchased allowance and return, and purchase discount
- ✓ Determine the net purchase from purchases subtracted purchase allowance and return, and purchase discount
- ✓ Add : Fright cost to inventory
- ✓ Determine the ending inventory

$1,000 Beginning inventory + $45,000 Purchases – Purchase Return $5,000 – Purchase discount $2,000+ Freight cost 1,500- $5,500 Ending inventory

= $35,000 Cost of goods sold

Step 3 : Calculate gross profit from sale revenue minus cost of goods sold

Step 4 : Calculate net income from gross profit minus expenses.

The following example shows the calculation of cost of goods sold under periodic inventory system. You will see the calculation that is different comparing with Perpetual Inventory System. Base on the example below, the highlighted areas indicate the calculation to determine the cost of goods sold.

Income Statement with Periodic Inventory System

XYZ Company

Income Statement

December 31, 201X

Sale Revenue				$100,000
Less: Sale Return and Allowance			($ 5,000)	
Sale Discount			(2,000)	(7,000)
Net Sale				**$ 93,000**
Cost of goods sold :				
Beginning inventory		$ 1,000		
Purchase	45,000			
Purchase allowance and return	(5,000)			
Purchase discount	(2,000)			
Net Purchase		38,000		
Freight Cost		1,500		
Cost of goods available for sale			$40,500	
Ending Inventory			(5,500)	
Cost of Goods Sold				**35,000**
Gross Profit				$58,000
Expenses				30,000
Net Income				**$28,000**

Step 1

Step 2

Step 3

Step 4

38

You also need to understand how to record each transaction under periodic inventory system. The following examples show the journal entries in a periodic inventory system. Remember that periodic inventory system requires the physical count to calculate the actual cost of the inventory on hand at the end of accounting period. It then subtracts this actual ending inventory cost to determine the cost of goods.

Periodic Inventory System Journal Entries

Under a periodic inventory system, inventory purchases are initially recorded in a purchases account with the following journal entries:

[1] Company records a purchase of $3,000 of merchandise from supplier A on account:

	Debit	Credit
Purchases	45,000	
Accounts payable		45,000

This transaction indicates that company purchase merchandise on credit and customers will pay later. It increases company liabilities by $45,000. When it paid, liabilities will decrease $45,000 and decrease cash by $45,000. On the other hand, company only recording the purchase into the purchasing account and determine the cost of goods sold after the inventory count at the end of accounting period.

[2] Company records $ 800 of freight cost associated with the delivery of inventory:

	Debit	Credit
Freight cost	1,500	
Cash		1,500

Based on this transaction, company recorded the freight cost as expense. It will use to determine the cost of goods sold after inventory count.

[3] Company records a sale of inventory for $10,000 on credit.

	Debit	Credit
Accounts receivable	10,000	
Revenue		10,000

This transaction indicates company sold the merchandise with $10,000. However, company only recorded total sale revenue. Cost of goods sold will be determined after inventory count.

[4] Company records a return purchase inventory of $ 5,000

	Debit	Credit
Account Payable	5,000	
Purchase return		5,000

[5] Company records a purchase discount

	Debit	Credit
Account Payable	2,000	
Purchase discount		2,000

Both transactions 4 and 5 indicates the purchase return and discount to reduce liability by returned inventory and discount offered by suppliers.

Advantage and Disadvantage of Periodic and Perpetual Inventory System

Under the period inventory is most useful for smaller business to maintain the minimal amount of inventory. However, it requires a physical inventory count to determine the cost of goods sold at the end of accounting period. The perpetual inventory system, it provides an up-to-date and accurate inventory on hand during each transaction.

CHAPTER FOUR

DEPRECIATION METHODS

Most companies have different types of investments to operate its business efficiency and effectively. It is important to know how to classify and record investment expenses into a company accounting system. Example as investment for building, machinery, property, it should be capitalized and allocated into the number of expected life as depreciation expenses. However, repair and maintain the machinery, fix the fence, repair the roof, it should record as common expenses in the year.

As a company decided to capitalize long-term investment, it has few different types of depreciation method to allocate investment expenses into the number of expected useful life. In fact, depreciation is defined as a noncash expense that reduce the value of asset as result of deteriorate. Depreciation also records in the income statement that can lower the company's reported income from revenue.

Depreciation Methods

[1] Straight-line method -- it spreads the cost of fixed assets evenly over its useful life

[2] Declining balance method -- it is also named as an accelerate method of depreciation. It results in higher depreciation expense in the earlier year of fixed assets.

[3] Sum of digit method -- depreciation expenses will add all years of the fixed assets expected useful life and factoring in which year are currently in, as compared to the total number of year.

[4] Units-of production method -- total estimate number of units of the fixed asset that will produce over it expected useful life, as compared to the number of units produced in the current accounting.

The following examples are used to illustrate each depreciate method to determine the allocation of fixed asset over its expected useful life.

Straight Line Depreciation Method

Straight-Line Depreciation Method will apply this formula "Cost – *Salvage / number of useful life*" to determine the depreciated value of asset and annual depreciation expenses.

Example:

Equipment purchased for $10,000, expected life is 5 years and estimates salve value $2,000.

Step 1: Calculate the depreciated value -- $100,000 - $2,000 = $80,000
      (Cost – Salvage Value)
Step 2: Determine the depreciation rate – 100 / 5 years = 20%
Step 3: Determine the annual depreciation accumulated depreciation
Step 4: Determine the accumulated depreciation
Step 5: Determine the Book Value

Year	Depreciated Value		Depreciation Rate	Annual Depreciation	Accumulated Depreciation	Book Value
1	$80,000	x	20%	16,000	16,000 *	$84,000 **
2	$80,000	x	20%	16,000	32,000	$68,000
3	$80,000	x	20%	16,000	48,000	$52,000
4	$80,000	x	20%	16,000	64,000	$36,000
5	$80,000	x	20%	16,000	**80,000 *****	**$20,000 *****

> *Must equal to the total investment value*

As the example showed above, the straight-line depreciation method is charged evenly over the life of fixed assets.

Each Column of Calculation from Straight-line Depreciation Table:

First column – Number year of useful life of an asset.

Second Column – Depreciated value ($100,000 - $20,000 = $80,000). It is distributed evenly in Straight-line method over the life of fixed assets.

Third Column – Depreciation rate (100 / 5 years = 20%) to be used to calculate annual depreciation. It is distributed evenly over the number of useful life.

Fourth Column – Annual depreciation is distributed evenly ($80,000 x 20% = $16,000).

Fifth Column -- Accumulated depreciation to determine the book value of asset based on the accumulated annual expenses. Please see the calculation below:

* Accumulated Depreciation
   Year 1 -- $16,000 = $16,000
   Year 2 -- $16,000 + $16,000 = $32,000
   Year 3 -- $32,000 + $16,000 = $48,000
   Year 4 -- $48,000 + $16,000 = $64,000
   Year 5 -- $64,000 + $16,000 = $80,000

Sixth Column – Asset of book value at the end of each year. Please see calculate:
** Book Value
   Year 1 -- $100,000 - $16,000 = $84,000
   Year 2 -- $ 84,000 - $16,000 = $68,000
   Year 3 -- $ 68,000 - $16,000 = $52,000
   Year 4 -- $ 52,000 - $16,000 = $36,000
   Year 5 -- $ 36,000 - $16,000 = $20,000

*** At the year 5, the accumulated depreciation and the last year of the book value must equal to the total value of investment asset $100,000 (Accumulate depreciation $8,000 + $2,000 salvage value).

Declining Balance Depreciation Method

Declining Balance Depreciation Method is also named as an accelerate method of depreciation. As mentioned before, it results in higher depreciation expense in the earlier year of fixed assets. Under declining balance depreciation method, you will use the beginning of book value instead of depreciated value to calculate the annual depreciation. In other word, the formula from straight-line depreciation method does not apply to declining balance depreciation method.

Example:

Equipment is purchased for $10,000, expected life is 5 years and estimates salve value $2,000.

Step 1: Determine the beginning of book value (initial cost of asset)
Step 2: Determine the depreciation rate: 100 / 5 years = 20%, we will double the depreciation rate to calculate the annual depreciation that we call "Double Declining Balance Method."
Step 3: Determine the annual depreciation
Step 4: Determine the accumulated depreciation
Step 4: Determine the Book Value

Year	Depreciated Value		Depreciation Rate	Annual Depreciation *	Accumulated Depreciation **	Book Value
1	$100,000	x	40%	40,000	40,000	$60,000
2	$ 60,000	x	40%	24,000	64,000	$36,000
3	$ 36,000	x	40%	14,400	78,400	$21,600
4	$ 21,600	x	40%	8,640	87,040	$12,960*
5	$ 12,960	x	40%	7,040 *	80,000	$20,000*

Must equal to the total investment value

* At the year 5, the accumulated depreciation $80,000 and the last year of the book value must equal the total value of investment asset ($100,000). Since the last year of book value is greater than the four year of book value. It will add the overpaid annual depreciation to equal the book value.

If the last year of book value lesser than the year 4 of book value, you will add the annual depreciation to determine the last year of accumulated depreciation and minus the annual depreciate from four year of book value to equal the book value as same as salvage value.

As the example showed above, the Declining Balance depreciation method is charged higher at the beginning of depreciate year and gradually lower over the life of fixed assets.

Each Column of Calculation from Double Declining Depreciation Table:

First column – It is number years of assets.

Second Column – It uses the beginning of book value that will carry over from the year-end of book value to next year as beginning of book value under Declining balance method.

Third Column – Depreciation rate (100 / 5 years = 20%; double the depreciation rate to 40%) to be used to calculate annual depreciation. It is distributed evenly over the number of useful life.

Fourth Column – It is annual depreciation. The annual depreciation will be decreased year-to-year to determine book value

Annual Depreciation
Year 1 -- $100,000 x 40% = $40,000
Year 2 -- $ 60,000 x 40% = $24,000
Year 3 -- $ 36,000 x 40% = $14,400
Year 4 -- $ 21,000 x 40% = $ 8,600
Year 5 – $ 12,960 - $20,000 = $ 7,040

Fifth Column -- It is accumulated depreciation to determine the book value of asset based on the accumulated annual expenses. Please see the calculation below:

* Accumulated Depreciation
  Year 1 -- $40,000 = $40,000
  Year 2 -- $40,000 + $24,000 = $64,000
  Year 3 -- $64,000 + $14,400 = $78,400
  Year 4 -- $78,400 + $ 8,640 = $87,040
  Year 5 -- $87,040 - $ 7,040 = $80,000

Remember: In order to keep the accumulated depreciation $80,000 and book value same as salvage value $2,000, annual depreciation will be calculated from last second years to minus salvage value ($12,960 - $20,000 = $7,040). In addition, the last year of the total accumulated depreciation plus last year of book value must equal with the total cost of investment.

Sixth Column – It is book value of asset at the end of each year. Please see calculate below:

** Book Value
  Year 1 -- $100,000 - $40,000 = $60,000
  Year 2 -- $ 60,000 - $24,000 = $36,000
  Year 3 -- $ 36,000 - $14,400 = $21,000
  Year 4 -- $ 21,600 - $ 8,600 = $12,960
  Year 5 -- $ 12,960 + $ 7,040 = $20,000

Sum-Of-The-Years Digits Depreciation Method

This Sum-of-the-years digits depreciation method takes the expected life of asset and adds together for each year. The sum of the years' digits would be obtained by adding each year together: $5 + 4 + 3 + 2 + 1 = 15$ or use the formula $n(n+1)/2$ [$5(5+1)/2 = 15$]. Then you take each digit to be divided by this sum to determine the percentage.

Example: Equipment is purchased for $10,000, expected life is 5 years and estimates salve value $2,000.

Step 1: Determine depreciated value ($100,000 - $20,000 = $80,000)

Step 2: Determine the depreciation rate (add each year together and divided by the sum)

Step 3: Determine the depreciated factor

Step 4: Determine annual depreciation expense

Step 5: Determine accumulated depreciation

Step 6: Determine book value

Year	Depreciated Value		Depreciation Rate	Annual Depreciation	Accumulated Depreciation	Book Value
1	$80,000	x	5/15	26,667	26,667	$73,333
2	$80,000	x	4/15	21,333	48,000	$52,000
3	$80,000	x	3/15	16,000	67,000	$36,000
4	$80,000	x	2/15	10,667	74,667	$25,333 *
5	$80,000	x	1/15	5,333 *	80,000	$20,000 *

Must equal to the total investment value

*The last year of annual depreciation is determinate from the last second year of book value minus the salvage in order to equal the total value of asset ($100,000).

As the example showed above, the Sum-of -year digits depreciation method changes over the life of fixed assets.

Each Column of Calculation from Sum-of-Digits Depreciation Table:

First column – Number years of asset

Second Column – Depreciated value ($100,000 - $20,000 = $80,000) distributed evenly in Sum of Year Digits method

Third Column – Depreciation factor $5+4+3+2+1 = 15$ or $5(5+1)/2 =15$) to be used to calculate annual depreciation. It is distributed evenly over the number of useful life.

Fourth Column – It is annual depreciation and distribute evenly

* Annual Depreciation
Year 1 -- $80,000 x 5/15 = $26,667
Year 2 -- $80,000 x 4/15 = $21,333
Year 3 -- $80,000 x 3/15 = $16,000
Year 4 -- $80,000 x 2/15 = $10,667
Year 5 -- $80,000 x 1/15 = $ 5,333

Fifth Column -- It is accumulated depreciation to determine the book value of asset based on the accumulated annual expenses.

 * Accumulated Depreciation

 Year 1 -- $26,667 = $26,667
 Year 2 -- $26,667 + $21,333 = $48,000
 Year 3 -- $48,000 + $16,000 = $67,000
 Year 4 -- $67,000 + $10,667 = $74,667
 Year 5 -- $74,667 + $ 5,333 = $80,000

Sixth Column – It is book value of asset at the end of each year.

** Book Value
   Year 1 -- $100,000 - $26,667 = $73,333
   Year 2 -- $ 73,333 - $21,333 = $52,000
   Year 3 -- $ 52,000 - $16,000 = $36,000
   Year 4 -- $ 36,000 - $10,667 = $25,333
   Year 5 -- $ 25,333 - $ 5,333 = $20,000

Remember: the last year of book value must be the same as the salvage value. The last year of the total accumulated depreciation plus last year of book value must equal with the total cost of investment.

CHAPTER FIVE

ACCOUNTING CLASSIFICATION AND RECORDING

A set of financial statements rely on accounting classification and recording. From Pervious chapter, we discussed about the "basic accounting equation" that is used to balance both side of transactions (Assets = Liabilities + Owners' Equity) or (Assets = Liabilities + Stockholders' Equity). It is important to know how different types of transactions to be classified and recorded into the debit or credit side, and how does it relate or affect the financial statements.

Debit and Credit

Debit and credit is designed to record of account transactions. Usually, you will see the abbreviation of debit (Dr.) and Credit (Cr.). However, the most accounting students have common wrong perception to interpret the Debit side and Credit side. In fact, debit side is not always increasing side, and credit side is not always decreasing side. We are only posting the transactions into the left side (Dr.) or right side (Cr.) based on each transaction. In order to record each transaction into an appropriate account, you have to understand the essential concept of Debit and Credit and the effect on the financial statements.

"Debit" and "Credit" has two basic components:

[1] Debit and credit either increases or decreases based on the transactions.
[2] It keeps the books in balance, (debit entry must correspond with credit entry that is called standard double-entry system or dual accounts.)

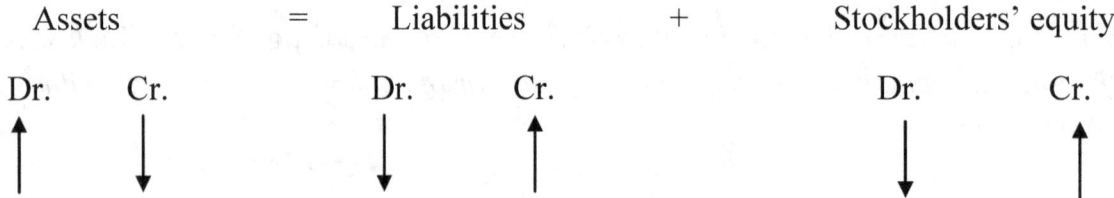

Assets		=	Liabilities		+	Stockholders' equity	
Dr.	Cr.		Dr.	Cr.		Dr.	Cr.

Referring the basic accounting equation, each category has debit and credit transactions. The diagram shows that [1] Assets increase are "debit" and decrease are "credit"; [2] Liabilities increase are "credit and decrease are "debit"; [3] Stockholders' equity increase are "credit" and decrease are "debit".

The diagram also explains how to record each transaction into the debit or credit side in order to fit in the basic accounting equation or balance the book. Please see detail explanation as follows:

The common rules of the journal entry related to the diagram are as follows :

Asset accounts - debit increases and credit decreases.

Assets Accounting

If assets increase, a transaction is posted into the Debit side. If assets decrease, it should be recorded under the credit side. The assets include Cash, Accounts Receivable, Notes Receivable, Inventories, Property, Plant and Equipment and other investments.

Liability accounts - credit increases and debit decreases

Liabilities Accounting

If a company increases liabilities, it should be recorded under the Credit side. It indicates that company obligates to repay current or non-current debts. When company repaid its liability, it reduces company's debt; it should be posted a transaction under the Debit side.

Revenue accounts - credit increases and debit decreases

For Expense accounts - debit increases and credit decreases (It reduce stockholders or owners' equity)

Stockholders' Equity

If the stockholders' equity increase from issuing more securities, and revenue, it is posted into the credit side. Decreasing the stockholders' equity by paying dividends, and expenses, it is posted into the debit side. However, expense accounts are posted to debit side to increase company's expenses and decrease owners or shareholders' equity.

In order to understand more of "debit" and "credit" transactions, following examples show how to record each transaction into the debit and credit side. You have to remember that all entries must keep in balance in the books. In the other words, when debit transaction recorded, it also needs to post it to the credit side, based on standard double-entry booking system.

Example of Transactions With Debit and Credit Entries

[Transaction one]

Company paid a rent for $3,500.

Dr. **Rent Expenses** **$3,500**
     Cr. **Cash** **$3,500**

(Debit rent expenses $3,500 to increase expenses and decrease cash.)

[Transaction Two]

Company purchased inventories for $10,000 on credit.

Dr. Inventory $10,000
 Cr.   Account Payable $10,000

(Debit inventory to increase a company current assets and credit account payable to increase a company's liabilities obligation to pay in short period of time.)

[Transaction Three]

Month Later, company will pay 40% of inventory cost from transaction two.

Dr. Account payable ($10,000 x 40%) $40,000
 Cr.   Cash $40,000

(Debit account payable to reduce liabilities obligation and credit cash to reduce company's current assets. After paying the partial amount of $40,000 liabilities as part of inventory purchasing, company still has $60,000 liabilities outstanding balance.)

[Transaction Four]

Company received cash $8,000 from customers for providing services.

Dr. Cash $8,000
 Cr.   Service Revenue $8,000

(Debit cash to increase a company current assets and credit service revenues to increase stockholders' equity or owners' equity.)

[Transaction Five]

Company provided services to a client for $1,000. Customer will pay on next month.

Dr.   Account Receivable $1,000
**   Cr.   Service revenue $1,000**

(Debit account receivable to increase current assets and credit service revenue to increase stockholders' equity or owners' equity.)

[Transaction Six]

Investors invested additional $30,000 for company's common stock.

Dr.   Cash $30,000
**   Cr.   Common Stock $30,000**

(Debit cash to increase current assets for exchanging company shares with investors. Also, company will credit common stock to increase stockholders' equity.)

[Transaction Seven]

Company paid dividend $500 to shareholders.

Dr.   Dividend $500
**   Cr.   Cash $500**

(Debit dividend to increase dividend paid to shareholders and credit cash to reduce company current assets.)

Now, you understand the concept of debit and credit transactions. You also need to know the recording process to prepare a set of financial statements. First, you have to know the difference between general journal and general entry. Second, you have to understand the purpose of a chart of account related to each entry.

GENERAL JOURNAL ACCOUNTS, GENERAL LEDGER ACCOUNTS, AND CHART OF ACCOUNTS

Today, most companies use different types of accounting software to record routine and non-routine transactions to prepare a set of financial statements. Moreover, the classification and recording is important in each transaction in order to post it into appropriate accounts. Moreover, you have to understand the processing how to post each transaction into general journal accounts and general ledger accounts with designed chart of accounts. It helps you to prepare qualify financial statements for a company.

General journal accounts are first to record all the daily transactions chronologically. It includes most common types of account: such as Cash, Accounts Receivable, Notes Receivable, Equipment, Accumulated Depreciation, Accounts Payable, Notes Payable, Sale / Service Revenue, Expenses and more. The next step is to transfer the daily transactions into an individual account as general entry accounts or t-accounts.

In fact, each account is assigned with special number to record each transaction, which is called as "Chart of Account." The number of chart of accounts is created to specify a list of all Assets, Liabilities, Equities, Revenue, and Expense and it varies depending on the size of the company. A small business may only have few chart of accounts and large company may have hundreds of chart of accounts to use to classify each transaction.

Example of Chart of Accounts:

Chart of Accounts:

	The first digit cannot change. You can add more digits after each designed chart of accounts

1	01-199 Asset Accounts
2	01-299 Liability Accounts
3	01-399 Equity Accounts
4	01-499 Revenue Accounts
5	01-599 Expense Accounts

Remember: the first digit cannot change. However, you can add more assets under the chart of accounts starting with 1, more liabilities starting with 2, more equities with 3, more revenue with 4 and expense with 5. Please see following examples to become familiar with each designed account.

Following are examples of asset accounts with assigned numbers of chart of accounts starting with "1":

Chart of Accounts	Asset Accounts
101	Cash
102	Account Receivable
103	Inventory
104	Short – term investment
105	Note Receivable
106	Prepaid insurance
110	Equipment
120	Property

Following are examples of liability accounts with assigned numbers of chart of accounts starting with "2":

Chart of Accounts	Liabilities Accounts
201	Account Payable
202	Insurance Payable
203	Note Payable
204	Salary Payable
205	Wage Payable
214	Short-Term Notes Payable
216	Unearned Revenue
220	Long-Term Notes Payable.

Following are examples of equity accounts with assigned numbers of chart of accounts starting with "3":

Chart of Accounts	Equity Accounts
301	Owner's Capital
302	Owner's Withdrawals
305	Common Stock
307	Common Stock - Dividend
308	Addition-Paid in Capital
309	Preferred Stock
310	Preferred Stock - Dividend
311	Retained Earnings
313	Treasury Stock

Following are examples of revenue accounts with assigned numbers of chart of accounts starting with "4":

Chart of Accounts	Revenue Accounts
401	Revenue
402	Interest Revenue
403	Other Revenue
405	Rental Revenue

408	Sale Returns and Allowances
409	Sale Discounts

Following are examples of expense accounts with assigned number of chart of accounts starting with "5":

Chart of Accounts	Expenses Accounts
501	Amortization Expense (Intangible Asset)
502	Depletion Expense (Natural Resource)
503	Depreciation Expenses (Tangible Assets)
508	Advertising Expense
509	Bank Charge Expense
511	Employees' Benefits Expense
512	Payroll Taxes Expense
513	Interest Expense
514	Insurance Expense
515	Rent Expense
516	Delivery Expense
517	Office Supplies Expenses
518	Salaries expense
519	Professional Expense
520	Bad Debts Expense
521	Wages Expense
522	Credit Card Expense
523	Repair Expense
524	Maintenance Expense
525	Truck Expense
526	General and Administrative Expense
527	Janitorial Expense
528	Miscellaneous Expense
529	Operating Expense
530	Property Taxes Expense
531	Postage Expense
532	Selling Expense

533	Telephone Expense
534	Traveling Expense
535	Utilities Expense

You might realize it why the number of chart of accounts do not consistence. The reason is that company might hold some spaces to create a familiar account transaction.

General Journal Accounts

General Journal accounts relate directly to a general ledger account. General Journal accounts are recording all day-to-day transactions. However, general ledgers are separate recording each transaction related directly to journal accounts and chart accounts. Now, assuming you are recording each transaction with assigned chart of accounts in each related entries as follows:

Chart of Accounts	Description	Debits	Credits
515	Rental Expenses	$3,500	$3,500
101	Cash		
	(company paid monthly rent)		
103	Inventory	$10,000	
201	Account Payable		$10,000
	(company purchased inventory on credit)		
201	Account Payable	$40,000	
101	Cash		$40,000
	(company paid outstanding balance to supplier)		
101	Cash	$8,000	
401	Service Revenue		$8,000
	(company provided services to customers)		

101	Cash	$30,000	
305	Common Stock		$30,000
	(Company issued common shares to exchange cash)		

T- ACCOUNTS (GENERAL LEDGER ACCOUNTS) AND NORMAL BALANCE

In order to determine the each account's normal balance from general ledger, we will look at a T-account from each of account classification to determine the normal balance. Normal balance is determined from the increasing side. Let us to use the basic accounting equation to define the normal balance as follows:

Assets	+	Liabilities	=	Stockholders' or Owners' equity
Debit – Increasing side		Debit –Decreasing side		Debit – Decreasing side
Credit – Decreasing side		Credit – Increasing side		Credit – Increasing side.

According to the table above, it depicts with basic accounting equation (Assets + Liabilities + Stockholders' or Owners' Equity). It shows the increasing side under the assets is on debit; increasing side under liabilities is on credit; and increasing side under stockholders or owners equity are on credit. You have to always remember that normal balance is under the increasing side.

T-account is divided by three sections that include Debit side, Credit side and Title Account. Following examples use T-account to find the normal balance.

Case 1:

Dr. ↑		Cash		Cr. ↓
	$			$
May 1	10,000	May 31		10,000
June 1	30,000			
Normal Balance	**30,000**			

Increasing company's cash on the months of May 1, *$10,000* and June 1, *$30,000* are posting into the debit side. Decreasing company's cash by the month of May 31, is posting into the credit side. Now, you take the total of the Debit (increasing) side minus the total of the credit (decreasing) side to arrive the normal balance *$30,000* under the debit (increasing) side.

Case 2:

Dr. ↑		Account Receivable		Cr. ↓
	$			$
May 1	14,000	June 25		20,000
June 1	30,000	July 20		10,000
July 1	35,000	Aug 28		10,000
Aug 1	25,000			
Normal Balance	**64,000**			

Company sold inventories on credit in the month of May 1, *$14,000*, June 1, *$30,000*, July 1, *$35,000* and August, *$25,000*. Also, customers started to pay the purchased inventories by the month of June, 25, *$20,000*, July 20, *$10,000* and August 28, *$10,000*.

Transactions recorded into the debit side to increase company current assets as accounts receivable with total $104,000. Later, collection from customers with total $40,000 recorded into the credit side to decrease company current assets as accounts receivable. Now, you take the total of debit (increasing) side ($104,000) minus total of credit (decreasing) side ($40,000) to arrive the normal balance $64,000. It is also an outstanding balance that will be collected from customers with short period of time.

Case 3:

Dr. ↑		Inventory		Cr. ↓	
	$				$
May 1	10,000	June 25			5,000
June 1	10,000	July 20			10,000
July 1	20,000	Aug 28			10,000
Aug 1	30,000	Sept 30			15,000
Normal Balance	**30,000**				

Company purchased more inventories from May 1, *$10,000*, June 1, *$10,000*, July 1, *20,000* and August 1, *$30,000*. It posted into the debit side to increase company inventories as current assets. Company also sold some inventories on June 25, *$5,000*, July 20, *$10,000*, August 28, *$10,000* and September 30, *$15,000* that posted into the credit side to decrease company inventories. You take the total of debit (increasing) side ($70,000) minus the total of credit (decreasing) side ($40,000) to arrive the normal balance $30,000.

Case 4:

Dr. ↓		Account Payable		Cr. ↑	
	$				$
May 1	10,000	June 25			20,000
June 1	10,000	July 20			30,000
July 1	15,000	Aug 28			25,000
Aug 1	15,000	Sept 30			25,000
		Normal Balance			**50,000**

Company bought materials or supplies on credit on May 1, *$10,000*, June 1, *$10,000*, July 1, *$15,000* and August 1, *$15,000*. It recorded the transactions into the debit side to increase company current liabilities as accounts payable. Company started to pay partial of payment on June 25, *$20,000*, July 20, *$30,000*, August 28, *$25,000* and September 30, *$25,000* that posted into debit side to reduce company obligation as current liabilities. You will take total of credit (increasing) side ($100,000) minus total of debit (decreasing) side ($50,000) to arrive the normal balance $50,000.

Case 5:

Dr. ↓		Revenue		Cr. ↑
	$		$	
May 1	0.00	May 31	10,000	
		June 30	5,000	
		Aug 28	15,000	
		Normal Balance	**30,000**	

Company shows the total earned revenue from May 31 *$10,000*, June 30 *$5,000* and Aug. 28 *$15,000*. It posted into the credit (increasing) side. Since the debit (decreasing) side does not have any recorded transactions, the normal balance is $30,000. It indicates to increase shareholders or owners equity.

Case 6:

Dr. ↓		Shareholders' Equity		Cr. ↑
	$		$	
May 1	0.00	May 31	15,000	
		June 30	25,000	
		Aug 28	35,000	
		Normal Balance	**75,000**	

When company issues more shares, it will post into the credit (increase) side to increase shareholders equity. The total normal balance is $75,000

Case 7:

Dr. ↑		Expenses		Cr. ↓
	$		$	
May 31	7,000			
June 30	5,000			
Aug 28	10,000			
Normal Balance	**22,000**			

Company shows the total expenses $22,000 under the debit (increasing) side. It reduces stockholders or owners equity and increase expenses of a company. Since it does not have any recorded transactions under the credit (decreasing) sign, the total normal balance is $22,000.

UNADJUSTED TRIAL BALANCE

After determining the normal balance in each account, next step to prepare the unadjusted trial balance. Unadjusted trail balance is created from a list of all general ledger accounts. Debit normal balance will post into debit column and credit normal balance will post to credit column of unadjusted trial balance. The purpose of trial balance is to prove the debit balance equal to credit balance. However, it does not mean that it does not have any errors because some transactions require an adjustment at the end of accounting period.

The following example shows unadjusted trial balance with Debit and Credit column that is transferred from each general ledger accounts or T-accounts. You can see that debit normal balance from general ledger accounts are posted into debit column and credit normal balance are posted into the credit column. In addition, the unadjusted trial balance includes two statements, which are income statement and balance sheet.

ABC Company
Unadjusted Trial Balance
January 31, 2013

Description	Debit	Credit
Cash	$ 39,000	$
Account Receivable	64,000	
Inventory	30,000	
Prepaid Insurance	---	
Plant, Property and Equipment	---	
Account Payable		50,000
Note Payable		---
Unearned Revenue		---
Common Stock		75,000
Revenue		30,000
Expenses	22,000	
Total	$ 155,000	$ 155,000

Section of Balance Sheet

Section of Income Statement

Debit equal Credit

Remember: the total debits and total credits balance must be equal. If it cannot be balance, it indicates that it has a mistake. You have to investigate or find the errors from general entries. It may be omitted the transactions or record transactions twice.

After preparing the unadjusted trial balance, we need to make an adjustment at the end of accounting period. When a company uses accrual basic, it records all transactions on book. It requires to make an adjustment to determine received income, paid expenses or others transactions in order to match income and expense in accounts.

Types of Adjustment Accounts

1] **Depreciation** – it is non-cash account, when a company invests in fixed assets, it requires to distribute an investment in number of useful life. Also, you have to make an adjustment to update the current depreciation expenses in income statement and book value in balance sheet.

2] **Prepaid Expenses** – it is a current asset of company to pay the expenses in advance. You have to adjust the current expenses to increase an expenses account and decrease the current asset as prepaid expenses.

3] **Accruals Revenue** – company has earned revenue, but not yet recorded and bill to customers. You need to make an adjustment to reflect the total accounts receivable and earned revenue in that period of time.

4] **Accruals Expenses** - it is a company current ability to pay in short period of time. It is recognized on balance sheet, such as interest expenses.

Example of adjusting entries:

[Adjusting Entry 1]

Company has beginning inventory $4,500. At the end of the accounting period, it only has $2,000 on hand. Company use $2,500 inventory. It requires making an adjustment to determine inventory expense and inventory on hand.

Dr.   Inventory Expenses $2,500 *   Cr.
Inventory $2,500

$2,500 = $4,500 - $2,000

[Adjusting Entry 2]

Company prepaid insurance for a year $24,000. It requires making an adjustment to reduce company current asset as prepaid insurance and increase insurance expenses. Since company prepaid a year with $24,000, it will divided the $24,000 by12 months = $2,000 a month.

Dr.	Insurance Expenses	$2,000
Cr.	Prepaid Insurance Expenses	$2,000

[Adjusting Entry 3]

Company accepted payment in advance as recording as unearned revenue from customer to remodeling the whole building $300,000. At the end of accounting period, company completed the part of project and realized $150,000 as earned income. It also requires to make an adjustment. This adjustment increase company income and reduce liabilities as unearned revenue.

Dr.	Unearned Revenue	$15,000
Cr.	Revenue	$15,000

[Adjusting Entry 4]

Company invested to equipment $10,000 with useful life 5 years and estimated salvage value is $1,000. This adjustment is contra accounting to increase depreciation expenses and accumulated expenses in both income statement and balance sheet.

Dr.	Depreciation Expenses	$2,000
Cr.	Accumulated Depreciation	$2,000

[Adjusting Entry 5]

Company pays salary biweekly $4,000 a month on Thursday. The next paycheck will overlap the current month and next month by 3 day from May 28, 20xx to June 8, 20xx. From the month of May, 28, 20xx, to June 8, 20xx, it has a day of salary expense recording in May, 20xx as part of salary expenses. It requires to make an adjustment $200 ($1000 / 5 days) as salary payable as obligation to pay employee at next pay check.

Dr.   Salary Expenses $200
   Cr.   Salary Payable $200

[Adjusting Entry 6]

Company borrowed $30,000 with interest 5% that requires to pay each month of $1,500 ($30,000 x 5%). This adjustment records the interest expenses and liability obligates to pay each month.

Dr.   Interest Expenses $1,500
   Cr.   Interest Payable $1,500

Adjusted Trial Balance

After making adjustments, you need to prepare adjusted trial balance to determine the amount of revenues and expenses. The purpose of adjusted trial balance is to calculate new account balance at the end of accounting period. In addition, adjusted balance will used directly to Balance Sheet and Income Statement.

Ten Columns Adjusted Trial Balance

Description	Unadjusted Trial Balance Debit	Unadjusted Trial Balance Credit	Trial Balance Debit	Trial Balance Credit	Adjusted Trial Balance Debit	Adjusted Trial Balance Credit	Income Statement Debit	Income Statement Credit	Balance Sheet Debit	Balance Sheet Credit
Cash	$ 315,000	$	$	$	$315,000				$315,000	
Account Receivable	64,000				64,000				64,000	
Inventory	30,000			2,500	27,500				27,000	
Prepaid Insurance	24,000			2,000	22,000				22,000	
PP&E (Net)				2,000	2,000					2,000
Account Payable		50,000				50,000				50,000
Salary Payable				200		200				200
Interest Payable				1,500		1,500				1,500
Unearned Revenue		300,000	15,000			285,000				285,000
Common Stock		75,000				75,000				75,000
Revenue		30,000		15,000		45,000		45,000		
Cost of Goods Sold			2,500		2,500		2,500			
Expenses	22,000				22,000		22,000			
Salary Expenses			200		200		200			
Prepaid Insurance Expenses			2,000		2,000		2,000			
Depreciation Expenses			2,000		2,000		2,000			
Interest Expenses			1,500		1,500		1,500			
Total	$ 455,000	$ 455,000	$23,200	$23,200	$458,700	$458,700	$30,200	$45,000		
Net Income							14,800			
							$45,000	$45,000		
Retained Earrings										14,300
									$428,000	$428,000

The totals of adjusted trial balance must be equal. Any difference indicates that there are some errors in the journal entries or others. The next step after the adjusted trial balance is to prepare the closing entries.

Closing entries are journal entries made at the end of accounting period, which transfer the balance of temporary accounts to permanent accounts. Temporary accounts are all accounts from income statement that includes Revenue, Income, Gain and Loss and expenses. Permanent accounts are all accounts recorded into the balance sheet. Remember, you only closed the temporary accounts and created the other income summary account for the closing process.

Closing Entries

Following examples of closing entries are based on the adjusted trial balance of ABC Company.

Date	Accounts	Debit	Credit
Jan 31	Service Revenue	$45,000	
	Income Summary		$45,000
Jan 31	Income Summary	$52,500	
	Cost of goods sold		$ 25,000
	Salary Expenses		22,000
	Prepaid Insurance Expenses		2,000
	Depreciation Expenses		2,000
	Interest Expenses		1,500
Jan 31	Income Summary	$14,300	
	Retained Earnings		$14,300

ACCOUNTING CYCLES

Following is major steps in accounting cycles. It shows the step-by-step process, including recording, classification, adjusting entries and closing entries.

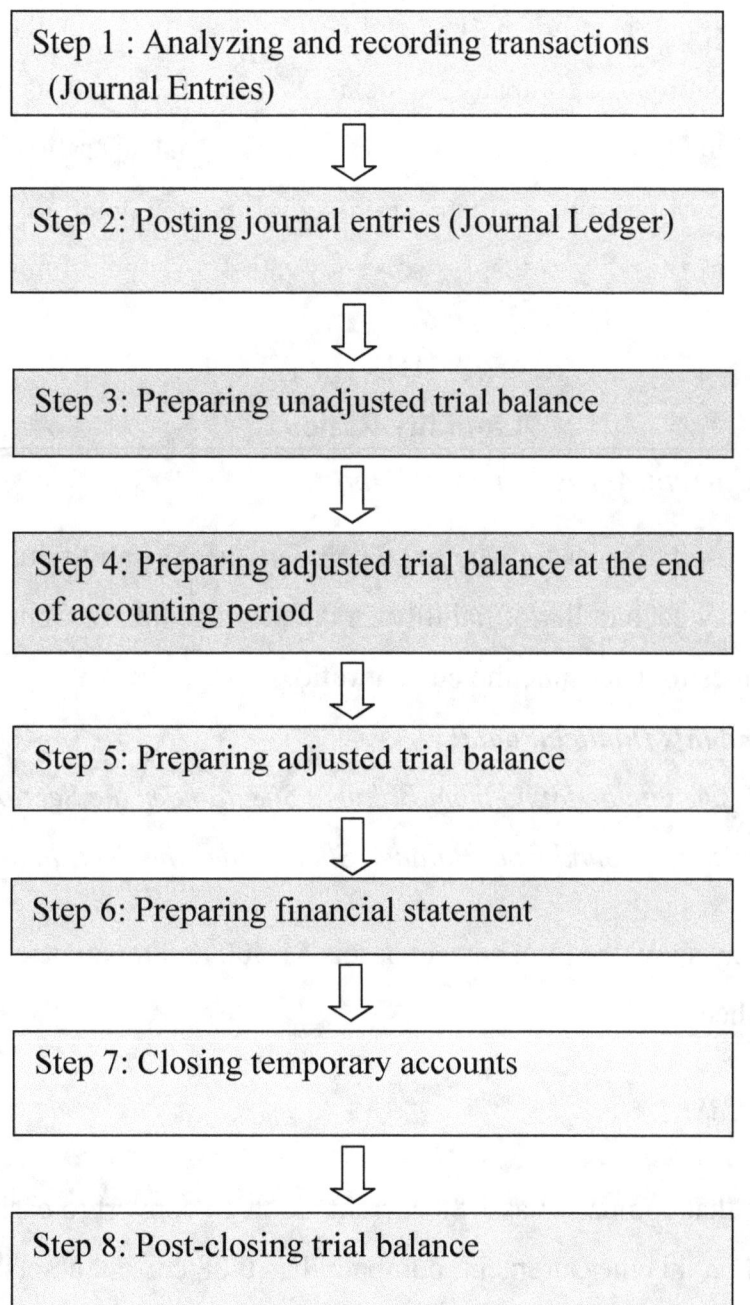

Step 1 : Analyzing and recording transactions (Journal Entries)

Step 2: Posting journal entries (Journal Ledger)

Step 3: Preparing unadjusted trial balance

Step 4: Preparing adjusted trial balance at the end of accounting period

Step 5: Preparing adjusted trial balance

Step 6: Preparing financial statement

Step 7: Closing temporary accounts

Step 8: Post-closing trial balance

CHAPTER SIX
ANALYSIS RATIO

Ratio analysis is important tools to measure a company financial situation or performance for decision-making. Although a set of financial statements provide a financial data of company's sales, profit and loss, total assets, total liabilities, and stockholders' equity, it may not clearly to express a company financial performance by the dollar amounts. In order to complete exanimate a company financial performance, analysis ratio can help a company to identify its financial strength and weakness. Analysis ratio can be defined with four major types of ratios to evaluate a company financial position. It includes [1] liquidity ratios, [2] profitability ratios, [3] solvency ratios, [4] operation ratios.

[1]
Liquidity Ratio

Current Ratio = Current Assets / Current liability

Current Ratio: it is used to measure whether a company has the ability to convert current assets into cash to pay each dollar of liability. You will take the total current assets divided total current liabilities to determine the current ratio.

Where can you find this financial data:

**Total Current Assets can be found from Balance Sheet under the Section of Assets.*

** *Total Liabilities can be found from Balance Sheet under the Section of Liabilities*

Example : Company show the total current assets $1,500 and total current liabilities $800 from the balance sheet.

$1,500 / $800 = 1.88: 1

The ratio indicates that company has 1.88 current assets to convert to cash to pay each dollar of liability. Based on this measurement, company has 0.88 current assets after pay each dollar of liability. Higher is the better. It indicates a company has enough current assets to be liquidated to a cash to pay the current liabilities.

Quick Ratio = Current Assets – Inventory / Current Liabilities

Quick Ratio is also used to measure how could be quickly to convert the current assets into cash without inventories. Inventory may be either less liquid than other current assets or loss its value. It depends on the type of industry or type of materials. You take the total current assets minus inventory divided by total current liabilities. The result of analysis will indicate does a company have sufficiency current assets to pay current liabilities without including inventory.

Where you can find this financial data:

** *Total Current Assets, Inventory from Balance Sheet under the Section of Assets*
** *Total Current Liabilities from Balance Sheet under the Section of Liabilities*

Example : Company shows the total current assets $1,500, inventory on hand $400, and total current liabilities $800 from the balance sheet.

$1,500 - $400 / $800 = 1.38: 1

Based on this measurement, company indicates 1.38 current assets to convert into cash to pay each dollar of liabilities without including inventory. After paying each dollar of liability, company still has 0.38 current assets on hand.

Remember: the result of this quick ratio measurement should be lower than the current ratio because it is excluding inventory.

Efficiency Ratios

Inventory Turnover

Inventory Turnover is used to measure how quick a company's inventory sold and replace over a period of time. You take the cost of goods sold divided by average total inventory.

Where you can find this financial data:

** *Cost of goods sold from the top of income statement under the revenue.*
** *Inventory from Balance Sheet under the Section of current assets.*

Example : Company shows inventory $30,000 in current year and $25,000 in prior year. Company also recorded cost of goods sold $15,000.

$15,000 / ($30,000 + $25,000) = 2.73

It indicates a company has 2.73 time inventory turnover ratio to fill customers need. The high is better.

Days' Sales in Inventory = 365 days / Inventory

It is also helpful to measure by using 365 days to show how long it takes to turn over its inventory.

Example : Day's sales in inventory = 365 days / Inventory turnover

365 days / 2.73 = 133.70 days

Based on the measure, company needs 133.70 days to turnover its inventory. The smaller number is more efficient to moving a company inventory.

Accounts Receivable Turnover = Net Sale / Accounts Receivable

Accounts receivable turnover is used to measure how quick a company to receive the outstanding balance from customers. You take net sale divided by average accounts receivable.

Where you can find these financial data:

** Net Sale from top of Income Statement

** Accountings Receivable from Balance Sheet under the Section of current Assets

Example: Suppose Company has net sale $3,500 and account receivable $2,000 in current and $1,000 from prior year.

$3,500 / ($2,000 + $1,000)/ 2 = 2.33 times

It indicates that company has outstanding accounting receivable equaled to the collection of accounting receivable of 2.33times over a year.

Days' Sales Outstanding = 365 days / Accounts Receivable Turnover

It is used to measure how many days needed to receive the outstanding accounts receivable from customers.

Example: account receivable turnover is 1.75time.

365 days / 2.33 times = 156.65 days.

It indicates that company needs 156.65 days to receive the outstanding balance from customers. If the measurement shows the higher result of days, it has more risk to receive the accounts receivable. Company may suffer from the loss of accounts receivable.

Accounts Payable Turnover = Total Purchase / Average Accounts Payable

This ratio is used to measure how quick of a company to pay off its suppliers. You take the total purchase divided average accounts payable.

Where you can find this financial data:
** Purchase from income statement.
** Accounts Payable from balance sheet under current liabilities.

Example: Company recorded total purchase $750,000 and average account payable $60,000 in current year and $57,000 from prior year.

$750,000 / ($60,000 + $57,000) / 2 = 12.82 times

It indicates a company has 12.83 times to payoff to suppliers. A higher ratio is more favorable than lower.

Days' Account Payable = 365 days / Accounts Payable Turnover

It is used to measure how many days needed to pay to the suppliers.

Example: account payable turnover is 12.82 times.

365 days / 12.82 times = 28.47 days.

It indicates that company needs 28.47 days to pay the outstanding balance to suppliers. Higher results of days, it indicate a company might face with financial difficult.

Assets Turnover Ratios = Net Sales / Total Assets

It measures the efficiency the management to use the total assets to generate the sale revenue. Higher the percentage provides more capacity to turn over from each dollar investment to produce sale revenue. You take net sale divided total assets.

Where can you find this financial data:

** *Net sale from income statement (usually take the sale revenue minus sale return and allowance and sale discount equal net sale)*

$$
\begin{array}{rl}
& \text{Sale Revenue} \\
- & \text{Sale Return and Allowance} \\
- & \text{Sale Discount} \\
\hline
= & \text{Net Sale} \\
\hline
\end{array}
$$

** *Total Asset from Balance sheet under the section of total assets which includes short-term and long-term assets)*

Example : Company reported the net sale $2,500 and Total assets $3,500

$2,500 / $3,500 = 0.71 times

According to the result of analysis, it indicates the efficiency to use the total asset to general sale revenue with 0.71 times.

Fixed Assets Turnover = Net Sales / Net Fixed Assets

This ratio is used to measure how a company invested fixed assets to general net sale. Fixed assets are holding from Company intent to resell or use to produce the products. Also, fixed assets should not be immediately expenses from income statement; it should be capitalized in number of useful life. The gain or loss will be realized by the time of disposal the fixed assets.

Where can you find this financial data:

** *Net sale can be found under income statement after the sale revenue minus sale return and allowance, and sale discounts.*

** *Fixed assets can be found under the balance sheet as long-term assets.*

The example of some fixed assets include as follows:

- o Equipment
- o Property
- o Building
- o Land
- o Machine
- o Vehicle

Example: Company has Net sale $3,000 and Net Fixed Assets $560

$3,000 / $560 = 5.36 Turnover per year

The result of analysis indicates that company generated $5.36 of sales from each dollar of net fixed assets. Higher is better to show a company can generate more sales for every dollar in fixed assets.

**Total Debt Ratio = Total Liabilities / Total Assets**

This ratio is used to measure the percentage of a company's assets that are financed by debt. If the ratio is higher than 50%, it can be interpreted that a company has 50% assets are financed by debt. Higher of this ratio is indicated that a company has higher leverage. You will take the total assets (including short term and long term) divided total liabilities (short term and long term)

**Where do you find this financial data:**

** Total Liabilities can be found from balance sheet that includes short-term and long-term liabilities.
** Total Assets also can be found from balance sheet that includes short-term and long-term assets.

Example : Company shows the total assets $2,500, and total liabilities $1,500 from balance.

$1,500 / $2,500 = 0.6 of 60%

This analysis indicates that a company has 60% debt of its 100% assets. In other words, a company has more than 50% debt that is financed to the business.

Debt-To-Equity Ratio = Total Debt / Total Equity

This ratio is used to measure a company's financial leverage from creditors, and suppliers. It shows a shareholders' equity can fulfill an obligation to creditors. You take the total debt divided the total equity.

Where you can find this financial data:

** *Total Debt (including short-term and long-term debt) can be found from balance sheet*

** *Total Equity can be found from balance sheet under stockholders' equity*

Example : Company shows total debt $80,000 and total equity $100,000

$80,000 / $$100,000 = 0.8

It shows that every dollar of company owned by the shareholders less than 1.00. It indicates that company has less leverage and stronger equity position.

Debt-To-Total-Asset Ratio = Total Liabilities / Total Assets

This ratio is used to measure a company's assets that are financed with loans. Company has obligation to pay for the outstanding loan. You take the total liabilities divided total asset.

Where can you find this financial data:

** *Total Liabilities from balance sheet (including L/T and S/T Liabilities)*
** *Total Assets from balance sheet (Including L/T and S/T Assets)*

Example: company shows the total liability $10,000 and total assets $18,500 from balance sheet.
$10,000 / $18,500 = 0.54

It indicates that a company has 0.54 long-term debts for each dollar of its assets. Usually, the measurement is over 0.5, it considers higher risk.

**Time Interest Earned = EBIT (Earnings Before Income Tax) / Interest Expenses**

This ratio is used to measure to a company ability to make interest payment in future. Sometime, this ratio is called Coverage Ratio. You take the earning before income tax divided interest expenses.

**Where you can find this financial data:**

** EBIT (Earnings Before Income Tax) can be found from income statement
** Interest Expense can be found from income statement before earning

Example: Company has earnings before income tax $56,000 and interest expenses $8,000

$56,000 / $8,000 = 7

It indicates that company can make enough income to pay the interest expenses 7 times over. In other words, company has earned income before income tax is 7 times higher to interest expenses.

<u>*Cash Coverage = EBITDA (Earning Before Income Tax , Depreciation and*</u>
<u>*Amortization / Interest Expense*</u>

This ratio is used to measure a company of cash available to pay for interest expenses. You take the EBITDA (Earnings Before Income Tax, Depreciation and Amortization)

Where you can find this financial data:

** *EBITDA can be found from income statement*
** *Interest Expense is also available from income statement*

Example: a company has earned income before tax, depreciation and amortization of $150,000 and depreciation $7,000 and amortization $5,000. Interest expense is $12,000.

$150,000 + $7,000 + 5,000 / $12,000

= $162,000 / $12,000

= 13.5

This result of this cash coverage analysis shows that a company can pay it interest expense comparing with same industry.

[3]
PROFITABILITY RATIOS

Gross Profit Margin = Net Sale – Cost of Goods Sold / Net Sale

Or

Gross Profit / Net Sale

This ratio is used to measure a company health financial situation after cost of goods sold.

Where can you find this financial data:

** *Gross Profit (Net Sale minus Cost of Goods Sold) from income statement*

** *Net sale can be found from income statement. If company has sales discount, sale return and allowance, it will take the revenue minus both to equal to net sale.*

Sale Revenue

- Sale return and allowance

- Sale discount

= *Net Sale.*

 - Cost of goods sold

= *Gross Profit*

Example : Company recorded the net sale $80,000 and Gross profit $35,000

$35,000 / $80,000 = 0.44%

It indicates that every dollar of a company earns, it only has 0.44% revenue to pay operating or other expenses.

Net Profit Margin = Net Income / Net Sale

This ration is used to measure every dollar of sale to derive in earnings. It is important to know how much earning can keep in each dollar of sale. You take the net income divided Net sale.

Where you can find this financial data:

* *Net Income can be found from the bottom of income statement*
* *Net Sale can also be found from the top of income statement*

Example : Company recorded Net sale $250,000 and Net Income $150,000

$150,000 / $250,000 = 0.6%

It indicates that a company has a net income of 0.6% from each dollar of sale.

Operating Profit Margin = EBIT (Earning Before Income Tax) / Net Sale

Or

Operating Income / Net Sale

This ratio is used to measure a company the operating income (before interest and taxes) on each dollar sale. Higher the profit margin, it indicates a company has a very healthy financial position.

Where can you find this financial data:

* *Operating Income (Earning before income Tax) can be found from income statement*
* *Net Sale also can be found from income statement*

Example : Company recorded the operating income $20,000 and net sale $ 45,000
$20,000 / $45,000 = 0.44%
This ratio result indicates that company has net profit margin of 0.44% for every dollar of sales.

83

Return On Asset (ROA) = Net Income / Total Assets

This ratio is used to measure a company efficiency based on each of dollar of invested asset. Also, it indicates how efficiency of manager uses company assets to generate profit.

Where you can find this financial data:

** *Net Income can be found from the bottom of income statement*
** *Total Assets (including short-term and long-term assets) can be found from the*
  balance sheet

Example : Company recorded total assets $30,000 and net income $14,500
$14,500 / $30,000 = 0.48%

The result of this analysis indicates that the amount of profit made based on a dollar of its assets. Higher of a return on assets shows a company's ability to generate more profits.

Return On Equity (ROE) = Net Income / Shareholders' Equity

This ratio is used to measure a company's efficiency to generate profit from shareholders' equity.

Where you can find this financial data:

** *Net income can be found from the bottom of income statement*
** *Total Equity can be found from the balance sheet under the shareholders' equity*

Example : company recorded net income $15,000 and shareholders' equity $350,000

$15,000 / $350,000 = 0.043 (4.3%)

This result indicates that company $0.043 of profit for every $1 of shareholders' equity and giving the stock an ROE of 4.3%. A company does not general earning growth by using shareholders' investment funds.

MARKET VALUE INDICATOR

Market value indicators are used to forecast market trends to measure the current gains and losses in stocks.

<u>**Earnings Per Share = Net Income / Shares Outstanding**</u>

It is used to measure a price of share of a company's proportion of profit allocated to each outstanding share of common stock. In this ratio, it is better to use average common shares to measure the EPS, since the common shares fluctuated.

Where you can find this financial data:

** *Net Income can be found from the bottom of Income Statement*
** *Shares Outstanding can be found from the balance sheet under the stockholders'*
   equity. This is NOT the amount of shareholders' equity. It is number of
   outstanding common shares.

Example : Company recorded net income $15,000 and outstanding common shares is 100,000 thousand shares.

You calculation is : $150,000 / 100,000 thousand shares = $1.5

This ratio indicates that a company earnings per share (EPS) is $1.5.

<u>Price-Earnings Per Share = Market Value Price Per Share / Earnings per share</u>

This ratio is used to measure a market value of a stock relative to a company's earnings per shares. It indicates the market is willing to pay for a stock on its current earnings. Since the market value is fluctuated, it can affect the price earnings per share.

Where you can find this financial data:

** *Market Value Price Per Share can be found from today stock value in market*
** *Earnings Per Share is coming from the EPS ratio*

Example: company has current market share is $65 per share and Earning Per Shares is $0.15

Your calculation is $65 / $1.5 = 43.33

A company R/E is 43.33 times. It indicates that investors are willing to pay $43.33 for every dollar of earning.

Market –to-Book Value (Price-to-Book Value) = Market Value of Equity Per Share / Book Value of Equity Per Share (Total Owners' Equity / Number of Shares Outstanding)

This ration is used to measure the market value of a company relative to a company book value. The difference between the market value and book value as follows:

Book Value also named as Historical Value. It is an initial value of investment. Market Value is current value of investment. It can be lower or higher than the book value.

Where you can find this financial data:

** Market Value of Equity Per Share as a company market capitalization that can be found from a company market profile.

** Book Value can be found from a company investment profile. Usually it is the book value or initial value of investment.

Example : Company recorded total owner's equity is $890 and number of share outstanding 600, market value $56 per share.

Your calculation is : $56 / ($890 / 600)
$$= \$56 / 1.48$$
$$= \$37.84$$

It indicates the market to book value is $37.84. If a value of stock is undervalued, the price is expected to rise. If it is overvalued, the price is expected to fall.

CHATPER SEVEN
COMMON SIZE AND COMPARATIVE ANALYSIS

We have a basic idea of ratio analysis from pervious chapter. This chapter will use common size and comparative analysis to analysis a company income statement and balance sheet.

Common size also calls Vertical analysis – it can use to analysis either income statement and balance sheet. The purpose of common size is displayed with percentage in each item. For example, each item of activity from income statement is shown as a percentage of total revenue to express as a percentage of sales, and on balance sheet, each item is show as a percentage of total assets.

Example of Common Size in Income Statement

Revenue :			Calculation
Sale/service revenue	$200,000	100%	
Expenses:			
Office supplies expenses	$ 1,300	0.0065	$1,300 / $200,000
Advertising expenses	6,000	0.030	$6,000 / $200,000
Depreciation expenses	1,000	0.005	$1,000 / $200,000
Rental expenses	10,000	0.050	$10,000 / $200,000
Utilities expenses	2,000	0.010	$2,000 / $200,000
Salaries and wages expenses	5,000	0.025	$5,000 / $200,000
Total Expenses	$ 25,300	0.1265	$25,300 / $200,000
Net Income	$174,700	0.8735	$174,700 / $200,000

Common size applies to income statement to show the 100% of revenue related to each operating expenses. Company has revenue $200,000 as a 100 percentage of earned revenue. It will take the total 100% of revenue to determine a percentage related to each operating expenses. According to the calculation, company shows the total expenses as percentage 12.65% and net income 87.35%. In other words, company spend 12.65% as operating expenses form total 100% of revenue and remind the 87.35% as a company net profit.

Example of Common Size in Balance Sheet

ASSETS		Percentage (%)	Calculation
Cash	$ 627,845	0.722	$627,845 / $869,845
Account Receivable	80,000	0.092	$80,000 / $869,845
Inventories	50,000	0.057	$50,000 / $869,845
Note Receivable	20,000	0.023	$20,000 / $869,845
Prepaid expenses	12,000	0.014	$12,000 / $869,845
Equipment (net)	80,000	0.092	$80,000 / $869,845
Total Asset	$ 869,845	100%	$869,845 / $869,845
LIABILITIES			
Account Payable	$ 35,000	0.040	$35,000 / $869,845
Note Payable	10,000	0.012	$10,000 / $869,845
Short-term Debt	30,000	0.035	$30,000 / $869,845
Long-term Debt	70,000	0.081	$70,000 / $869,845
STOCKHOLDER'S EQUITY			
Common Shares	$ 200,000	0.23	$200,000 / $869,845
Retained Earning	524,700	0.60	$524,700 / $869,845
Total Liabilities and Stockholder's Equity	$ 869,845	100%	$869,845 / $869,845

When you applied the common size to the balance sheet, it indicates the total asset, total liabilities and stockholders' equity as 100% related to each transaction as a percentage. Based on the total of 100% asset, company has 72.7% from 100% of cash on hand. However, the 100% of the total liabilities and stockholders' equity shows 60% to retained earnings, 23% of common shares and 17% of total liabilities.

The advantage by using common size to analyze a company financial performance, it will give you a quick understanding of a company financial situation as a percentage of total revenue, total assets, total liabilities and stockholders' equity.

Company can use comparative analysis for income statement and balance sheet. It will compare its financial performance from a prior to current year to reflect a change in percentage.

Example of Comparative Analysis in Income Statement

Revenue :	Year 2	Year 1	Different	% change of Income Statement
Sale/service revenue	$200,000	$140,000	$60,000	0.43
Expenses:				
Office supplies expenses	$ 1,300	$ 1,000	300	0.30
Advertising expenses	6,000	2,500	3,500	1.40
Depreciation expenses	1,000	1,000	0.00	0.00
Rental expenses	10,000	8,000	2,000	0.25
Utilities expenses	2,000	1,500	500	0.33
Salaries and wages expenses	5,000	5,000	0.00	0.00
Total Expenses	$ 25,300	$ 19,000	6,300	0.33
Net Income	$174,700	$121,000	53,700	0.44

Company used the comparative analysis to analyze it two years financial situation with percentage changed. We can see that a company has revenue grow by 43% within 2 years and net income indicates 44% increased. By using comparative analysis in this income statement, it divided with five columns. First column is transaction, column two is current year of financial data, column three is prior year of financial data, and last column is percentage change of income statement. The breakdown of calculation to determine the percentage change of income statement as follows:

Percentage change of income statement = Current Year – Prior Year / Prior Year

1] Sale / Service Revenue

$200,000 - $ 140,000 = $60,000

= $60,000 / $140,000

= 0.43

2] Office Supplies Expenses

$1,300 - $1,000 = $300

= $300 / $1,000

= 0.30

3] Advertising Expenses

$6,000 - $2,500 = $3,500

= $3,500 / $2,500

= 1.4

4] Depreciation Expenses

$1,000 - $1,000 = $0.00

= $0.00 / $1,000

= 0.00

5] Rental Expenses

$10,000 - $8,000 = $2,000

$$= \$2,000 / \$8,000$$

$$= 0.25$$

6] Utilities Expenses

$2,000 - $1,500 = $500

$$= \$500 / \$1,500$$

$$= 0.33$$

7] Salaries and Wages Expenses

$5,000 - $5,000 = $0.00

$$= \$0.00 / \$5,000$$

$$= 0.00$$

8] Net Income

$174,700 - $ 121,000 = $53,700

$$= \$53,700 / \$121,000$$

$$= 0.44$$

Example of Comparative Analysis in Balance Sheet

	Year 2	Year 1	Different	% change of Balance Sheet
ASSETS				
Cash	$ 627,845	$620,500	$ 7,345	0.012
Account Receivable	80,000	60,000	20,000	0.333
Inventory	50,000	40,000	10,000	0.250
Note Receivable	20,000	18,500	1,500	0.081
Prepaid Expenses	12,000	13,000	(1,000)	(0.077)
Equipment (net)	80,000	70,000	10,000	0.143
TOTAL ASSETS	**$869,845**	**$822,000**	**$47,845**	0.058
LIABILITIES				
Account Payable	$ 35,000	$ 25,000	$10,000	0.400
Note Payable	10,000	8,000	2,000	0.250
Short-Term Debt	30,000	20,000	10,000	0.500
Long-Term Debt	70,000	49,000	21,000	0.429
TOTAL LIABILITIES	**$145,000**	**$102,000**	**$ 43,000**	0.423
STOCKHOLDER'S EQUITY				
Common Shares	$200,000	$200,000	$ 0.00	0.000
Retained Earning	524,845	520,000	4,845	0.009
TOTAL STOCKHOLDERS' EQUITY	**$724,845**	**$720,000**	**$ 4,845**	0.007
TOTAL LIABILITIES AND STOCKHOLDERS' EQUITY	**$869,845**	**$822,000**	**$ 47,845**	0.058

By using the comparative analysis from this balance sheet, it shows the percentage of change from two years financial data. It is easy to understand a company financial position in the two years business operation. Account receivable increases by 33% and account payable increases by 44%. It may indicate that a company has 33% outstanding balance from customers and owe the suppliers for 44%.

The calculation is same as the income statement by applying the comparative analysis. You will take the current year minus prior year equal a different and take the different divided to prior year.

[1] Cash

$$\$627,845 - \$620,500 = \$7,345$$
$$= \$7,345 / \$620,500$$
$$= 0.012$$

[2] Account Receivable

$$\$80,000 - \$60,000 = \$20,000$$
$$= \$20,000 / \$60,000$$
$$= 0.333$$

[3] Inventory

$$\$50,000 - \$40,000 = \$10,000$$
$$= \$10,000 / \$40,000$$
$$= 0.250$$

[4] Note Receivable

$$\$20,000 - \$18,500 = \$1,500$$
$$= \$1,500 / \$18,500$$
$$= 0.081$$

[5] Prepaid Expenses

$12,000 - $13,000 = ($1,000)

= ($1,000) / $13,000

= (0.077)

[6] Equipment (net)

$80,000 - $70,000 = $10,000

= $10,000 / $70,000

= 0.143

[7] Total Liabilities

$145,000 - $102,000 = $43,000

= $43,000 / $102,000

= 0.423

[8] Account Payable

$35,000 - $25,000 = $10,000

= $10,000 / $25,000

= 0.400

[9] Note Payable

$10,000 - $8,000 = $2,000

= $2,000 / $8,000

= 0.250

[10] Short-Term Debt

$30,000 / $20,000 = $10,000

= $10,000 / $20,000

= 0.500

[11] Long-Term Debt

$70,000 - $49,000 = $21,000

$$= \$21,000 / \$49,000$$
$$= 0.429$$

[12] Total Liabilities

$145,000 - $102,000 = $43,000

$$= \$43,000 / \$102,000$$
$$= 0.423$$

[13] Common Shares

$200,000 / $200,000 = $0.00

[14] Retained Earning

$524,845 - $520,000 = $4,845

$$= \$4,845 / \$520,000$$
$$= 0.009$$

[15] Total Stockholders' Equity

$724,845 - $720,000 = $4,845

$$= \$4,845 / \$720,000$$
$$= 0.007$$

[16] Total Liabilities and stockholders' Equity

$869,845 - $822,000 = $47,845

$$= \$47,845 / \$822,000$$
$$= 0.058$$

Now, you should have a basic ideal and concept how to structure and read a company's financial statements. Although you know how to apply different type of ratio to analyze a company financial performance, it is important to understand how to interpret a set of financial statements meaningful, which include income, balance sheets and cash flow statement.

ABOUT THE AUTHOR

I was teaching in SUNY University as adjunct in business department for 12 years. Currently, I am employed as full-time professor in private college to teach MBA students in Business Department. My major teaching areas include financing and accounting.

I also earned my doctoral degree with Executive Leadership and Technology, MBA in International Banking and Financing, Bachelor in Accounting. I had been working in the accounting filed for more than 8 years. According to the number years of my teaching careers in financing and accounting, and working experiences, I would like to share some of basic accounting concepts with students or others who are interesting in accounting or financing field. In addition, I will continue to explore more concepts to share with everybody. Hope you will enjoy this book. Thank you very much for your reading.